HANDY REFERENCE

Absolute URL
The Uniform Resource Locator for a Web page. It must include the host name, directory and file name. E.g.:
http://www.computerstep.com/index.html

Bit depth
A bit is a binary digit, either a 1 or a 0. A number of bits can be used to represent a colour. More bits mean more colours can be used.

CGI script
Common Gateway Interface. Specialised programs that run on a server in response to input from a Web page. CGI scripts can pass on for instance the information you asked for in a form on your Web site.

Child Web
Any Web other than the Root Web on a server.

FTP
File Transfer Protocol. This is a set of agreed programming commands that allow data to be downloaded from a Web site.

GIF
Graphics Interchange Format. A standard graphic format on the Internet. Used for images that don't need to be of photographic quality. Allows up to 256 colours, one of which may be transparent.

HTML
HyperText Markup Language. The programming language of the Internet.

Hypertext
Some text that you see on Web pages is in a different colour – usually purple or blue. Clicking on this text will move you to another Web site. The text is hyper-linked to the information it refers to.

ISP
Internet Service Provider. Also known as Internet Access Providers. They usually provide the servers that Web pages are stored on. These servers make up the World Wide Web, as they are all connected together.

IP Address
Internet Protocol Address. A series of numbers separated by full stops that identify a computer connected to a network. For example, 165.156.55.78

JPEG
Joint Photographic Expert Group. Used when high-quality images are needed on a Web site. They have 24-bit pixel colour depth.

URL
Uniform Resource Locator. The address of a resource on the Internet. There are FTP URLs and also HTTP URLs, which link to Web pages.

ABOUT THE SERIES

In easy steps series is developed for time-sensitive people who want results fast. It is designed for quick, easy and effortless learning.

By using the best authors in the field, combined with our in-house expertise in computing, this series is ideal for all computer users. It explains the essentials simply, concisely and clearly - without the unnecessary verbal blurb. We strive to ensure that each book is technically superior, effective for easy learning and offers the best value.

Learn the essentials **in easy steps** - accept no substitutes!

Titles in the series include:

Operating Systems
Windows 95	1-874029-28-8

Applications - Integrated
Microsoft Office	1-874029-37-7
Microsoft Office 97	1-874029-66-0
Microsoft Works	1-874029-41-5
SmartSuite (97)	1-874029-67-9

Applications - General
Access	1-874029-78-4
Excel	1-874029-69-5
PowerPoint	1-874029-63-6
Word	1-874029-39-3
Word 97	1-874029-68-7
WordPerfect	1-874029-59-8

Accounting and Finance
Microsoft Money UK	1-874029-61-X
Quicken UK	1-874029-71-7
Sage Instant Accounting	1-874029-44-X
Sage Sterling for Windows	1-874029-79-2

Internet
CompuServe UK	1-874029-33-4
FrontPage	1-874029-60-1
HTML	1-874029-46-6
Internet Explorer	1-874029-58-X
Internet UK	1-874029-73-3
Netscape Navigator	1-874029-47-4

Graphics and Desktop Publishing
CorelDRAW	1-874029-72-5
PageMaker	1-874029-35-0
PagePlus	1-874029-49-0
Publisher	1-874029-77-6

Development Tools
Visual Basic	1-874029-74-1
Visual J++	1-874029-75-X

Hardware
Upgrading Your PC	1-874029-76-8

For credit card sales and volume discounts Tel: 01926 817999 or EMail: sales@computerstep.com

For international orders and rights Fax: +44 1926 817005 or EMail: sevanti@computerstep.com

EMail your reader comments to: harshad@computerstep.com

Visit our web site at http://www.computerstep.com

FRONTPAGE
in easy steps

Dave Howell

COMPUTER STEP

In easy steps is an imprint of Computer Step
Southfield Road . Southam
Warwickshire CV33 OFB . England

Tel: 01926 817999 Fax: 01926 817005
http://www.computerstep.com

First published 1997

Copyright © 1997 by Computer Step. All rights reserved. No part of this book may be reproduced or transmitted in any form or by any means, electronic or mechanical, including photocopying, recording, or by any information storage or retrieval system, without prior written permission from the publisher.

Notice of Liability

Every effort has been made to ensure that this book contains accurate and current information. However, Computer Step and the author shall not be liable for any loss or damage suffered by readers as a result of any information contained herein.

Trademarks

Microsoft® and Windows® are registered trademarks of Microsoft Corporation. All other trademarks are acknowledged as belonging to their respective companies.

Printed and bound in the United Kingdom

ISBN 1-874029-60-1

Contents

1. Getting Started 7
Installing FrontPage 8
Uninstalling FrontPage 12
Starting FrontPage 13
Creating a Web Site 14

2. The Explorer 21
Viewing Your Site 22
Changing the View 25
Hyperlink View 27
Folder View 31
Importing Documents 33
Deleting a Web Site 34
Changing Web Settings 35
    Parameters 35
    Configuration 37
    Advanced 38
    Language 39
Changing Your Password 40
Verifying Your Links 41
Configuring Editors 42
Permissions 45
    Administrator 47
    Author 48
    End User 48

3. The Editor 49
Starting the Editor 50
The Toolbar 51
Tables 54
Comments 57
Marquee Tags 58

Text	58
Direction	58
Movement Speed	59
Behaviour	59
Align With Text	59
Size	59
Specify Width/Height	59
Repeat	60
Background Color	60
HTML Commands	61
Original	61
Current	61
Show Color Coding	61
The To Do List	64
Task	64
Assigned To	64
Priority	64
Completed	64
Linked To	65
Description	65
Do Task	65
Details	65
Complete	66
Add	66
Frames	67
Creating a Custom Frame	70
Text Files	73
One formatted paragraph	75
Formatted paragraphs	75
Normal paragraphs	76
Normal paragraphs with line breaks	76

4. Wizards and Templates 77

Page Templates	78
Custom Templates	79
Wizards	81
Page Wizards	81
Web Templates	87

5. Designing Your Pages 89
    Text 90
    Page Properties 92
    Opening Pages 93
    Images 95
    Image Properties 97
    Video 98
    Hotspots 99
    Transparent Colours 101
    Sound 102

6. WebBots 103
    Introduction 104
        Client Bots 104
        Server Bots 104
    Search WebBot 105
        Label for Input 106
        Width in Characters 106
        Label for "Start Search" Button 106
        Label for "Clear" Button 106
        Word List to Search 106
        Score 106
        File Date 107
        File Size 107
    Scheduled Image/Include WebBot 108
    Substitution WebBot 110
        Adding a variable 111
    Table of Contents WebBot 114
    Timestamp WebBot 117
        Edited 118
        Updated 118
    Registration WebBot 119

7. Forms and Fields 121
    Form Page Wizard 122
    Form Fields 127
    Field Types 129
        One-Line Text Box 129

    Scrolling Text Box 129
    Check Box 129
    Radio Button 130
    Drop-Down Menu 130
    Push Button 130
  Field Validation 131
    Display Name 132
    Text Format 132
    Numeric Format 133
    Data Length 133
    Data Value 134
  Form Properties 135
  Configuring a Handler 137

8. The Personal Web Server 139

  The Personal Web Server 140
  Server Extensions 141
    Platforms 141
    Commercial Web Servers 141
    Non-commercial Web Servers 141
  The Server Administrator 142
    Install 142
    Uninstall 143
    Check 143
    Authoring 144
  Publishing Your Web Site 145
  Publish FrontPage Web 145
  FTP 148
    Transfer 148
    Don't transfer 148
  FrontPage Publishing Wizard 149

Index 155

CHAPTER ONE

Getting Started

In this chapter you will learn how to start FrontPage and use a Wizard to set up a Web site that you can use to try out the main features of FrontPage.

Covers

Installing FrontPage 8

Uninstalling FrontPage 12

Starting FrontPage 13

Creating a Web Site 14

Installing FrontPage

FrontPage uses the now familiar installation Wizard to take you step-by-step through the process. On inserting the CD-ROM into your computer you will see a screen that allows you to choose which programs to install onto your hard drive.

As you are dealing with the Internet, you also have a few other choices that you need to make as you move from screen to screen in the installation Wizard. As you can see, each entry is checked against the programs that are already on your hard drive. If they are already there – you may for instance be using Internet Explorer as your Web browser – you will be told so with a note in brackets under each option. You can therefore see instantly what you can, and need to, install.

You should be comfortable with Wizards if you have been using Windows for some time. You can set up FrontPage in one session if you have decided which elements you will need. Consider if you will be publishing your Web on an Intranet and wish to use the Personal Web Server. Also, if you are going to use Web space on a remote server, check that they have the Server Extensions that give FrontPage its special functions.

FrontPage in easy steps

...contd

You will see some preliminary dialogue boxes before you arrive at this one:

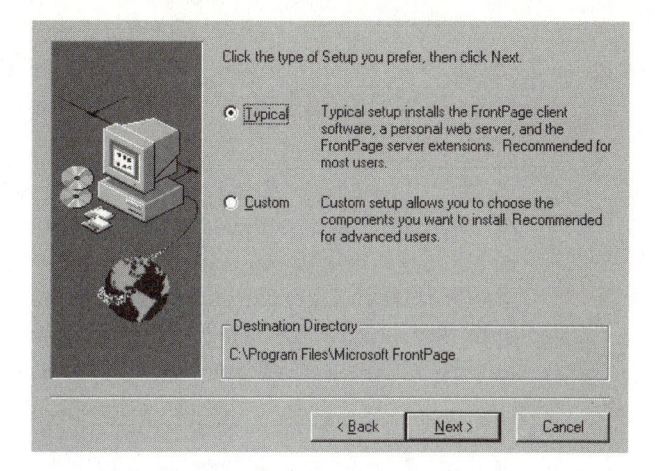

The Typical installation option will suit most users. You may however decide that you will not need certain components. If this is the case then choosing the Custom option will open this dialogue box:

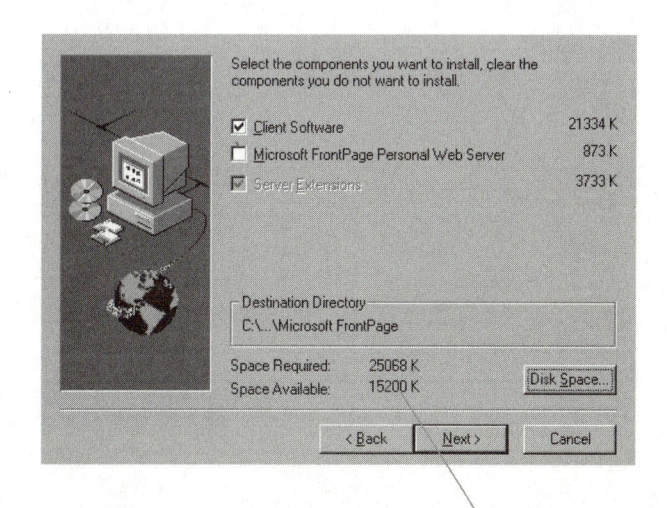

If you are short of hard disk space, you can see instantly how much space you will need to install each component.

1. Getting Started

...contd

If you do not intend to use your computer as a Web host, you do not need to install the Personal Web Server. You may however wish to install this to test your Web site as you build it. The Personal Web Server isn't intended to be used as a World Wide Web server, as it is for low-volume use only. It could however be used as the sole server on a small Intranet.

If you plan to use your computer as a host, but use a server other than the Personal Web Server provided, then you will need to install the server extensions. You must however check that the server that you use has the FrontPage server extensions running in it to make full use of the unique features that FrontPage offers, such as its WebBots.

When you have finished entering information into the dialogue boxes of the installation Wizard, you will see this screen. You will now have a chance to check the components that you are about to install and the directory they will be written to. If you want to change any of these settings, click 'Back' until you reach the dialogue box where you can make the changes.

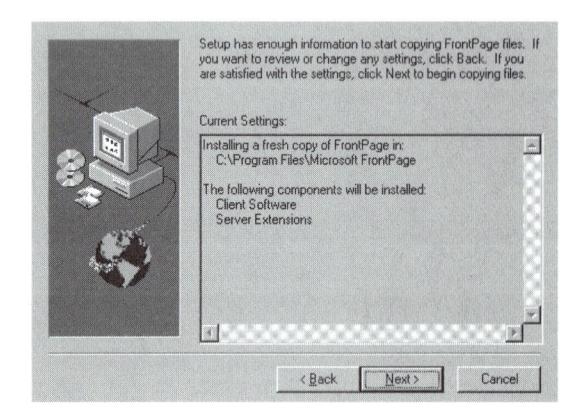

...contd

If all has gone well and FrontPage has installed all the necessary files on your hard drive, you should see this dialogue box open to confirm this. You can now start FrontPage from this dialogue box and begin to create your Web site.

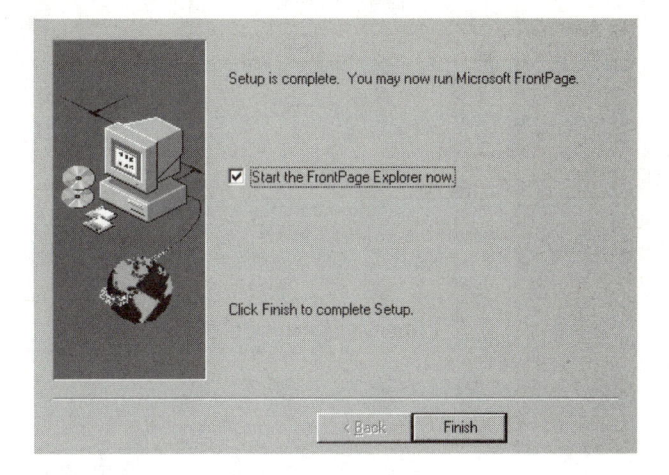

If you decided not to install some of the components that are contained on the CD-ROM at this time, you can install them when you are ready. They will simply be added to your hard drive, in the correct directory.

Uninstalling FrontPage

If for any reason you wish to uninstall FrontPage, you can do this from within Windows itself. If you open the Control Panel from the Settings level of the Start menu, you will see this window.

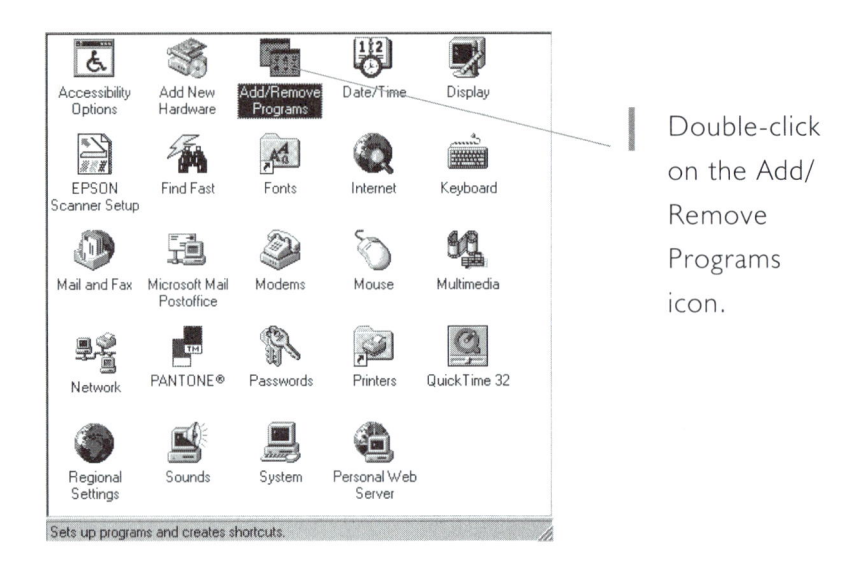

1 Double-click on the Add/Remove Programs icon.

You will see this window open. Now do the following:

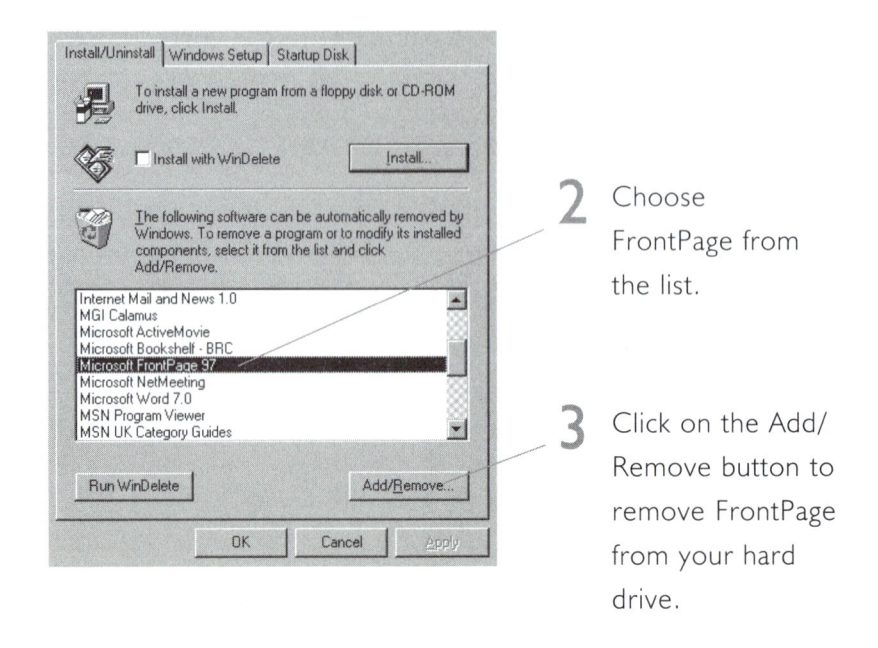

2 Choose FrontPage from the list.

3 Click on the Add/Remove button to remove FrontPage from your hard drive.

FrontPage in easy steps

Starting FrontPage

Each time you start FrontPage you will see this dialogue box appear, allowing you to perform the following tasks:

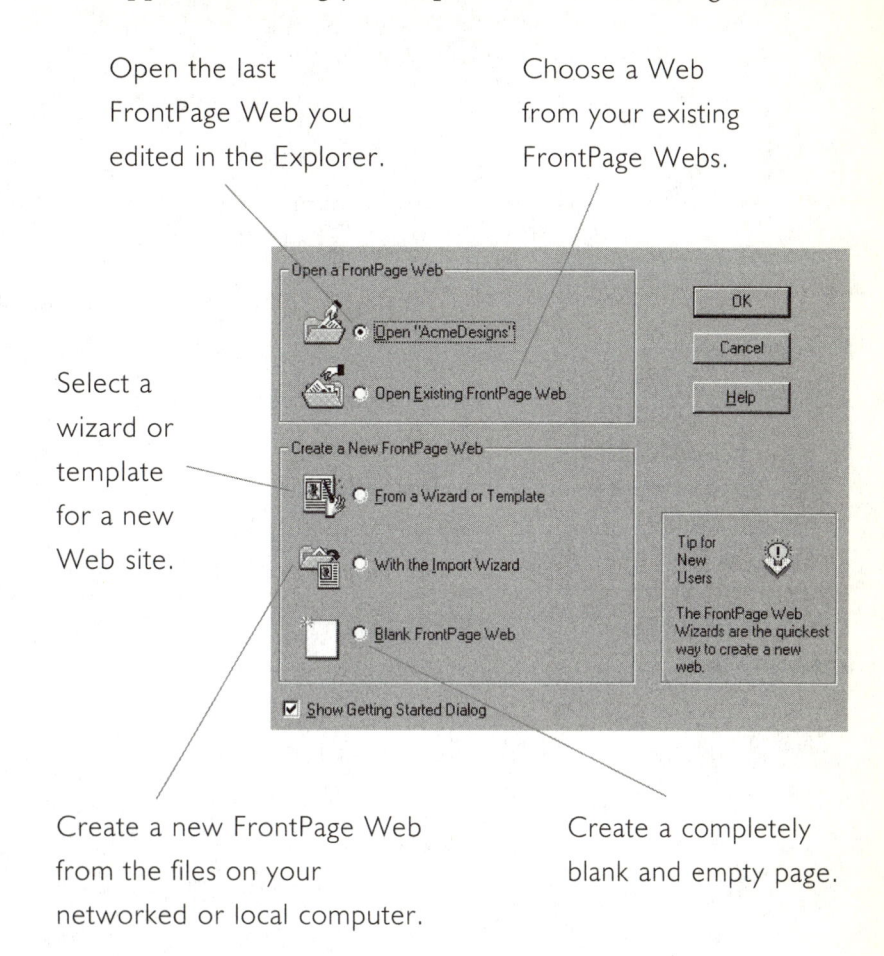

Open the last FrontPage Web you edited in the Explorer.

Choose a Web from your existing FrontPage Webs.

Select a wizard or template for a new Web site.

Create a new FrontPage Web from the files on your networked or local computer.

Create a completely blank and empty page.

1. Getting Started   13

Creating a Web Site

In this example the Corporate Presence Web site template is used. If you want to use another template to create a Web site, choose one from the list.

1. Start FrontPage to produce the initial dialogue (see the previous page).

2. Select 'From a Wizard or Template', then click OK.

3. The Template or Wizard dialogue appears. Highlight the Corporate Presence Wizard, or any of the Wizards you want to try out, and click OK.

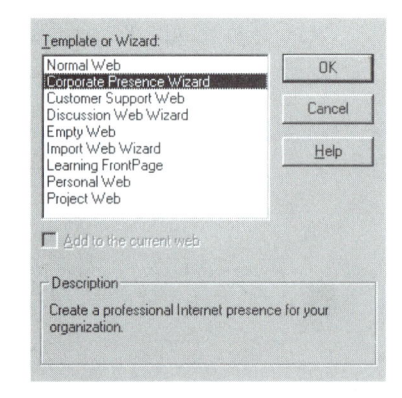

BEWARE: Passwords and Web names are case-sensitive. Be careful to remember how you entered this information.

4. Give your new Web site a name and choose a password.

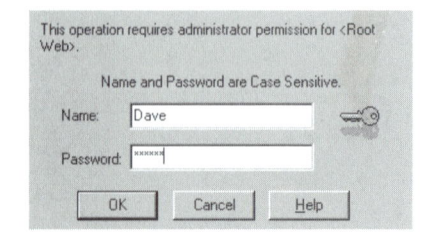

5. This is the first screen of the Corporate Presence Wizard. Click on Next to move to the next screen.

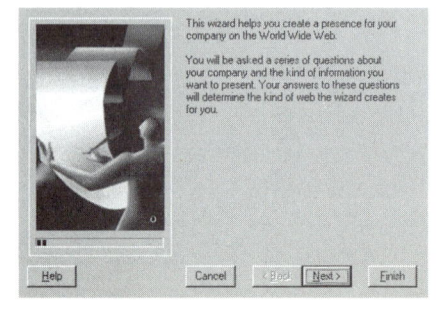

14   FrontPage in easy steps

...contd

6 Enter the location of your server and the name of your Web site.

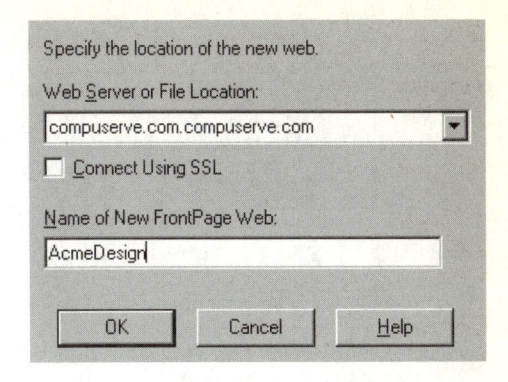

7 Click on all the options that you want to build into your Web site.

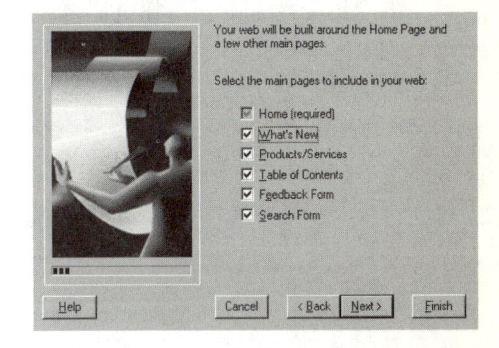

8 Select all those topics you want to include in your Web site.

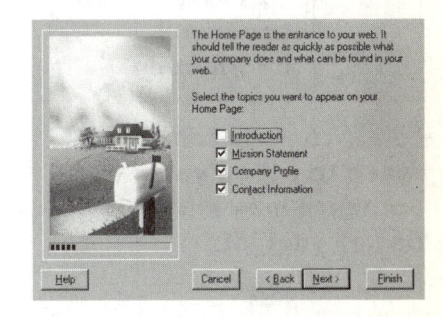

9 Choose how you are going to keep your customers or visitors informed.

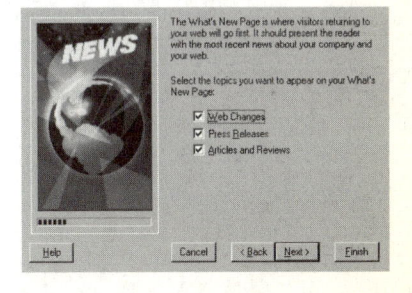

1. Getting Started

...contd

10 Choose how many products and/or service pages you want FrontPage to create on your Web site.

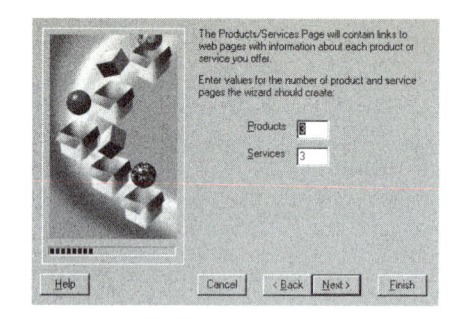

11 Here you choose how the products or services you entered in the last screen are to be displayed. Tick all that are appropriate.

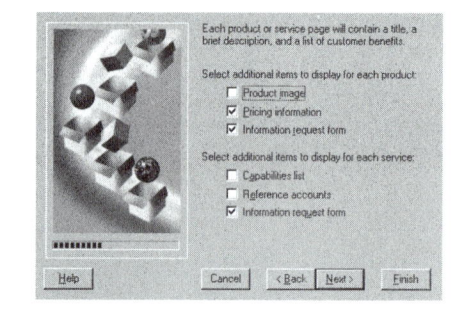

BEWARE

Be careful how much information you ask for. If there is too much to fill in, your audience may click out of your site.

12 This is where you create your feedback form. Think carefully about your audience, and what information you want from them.

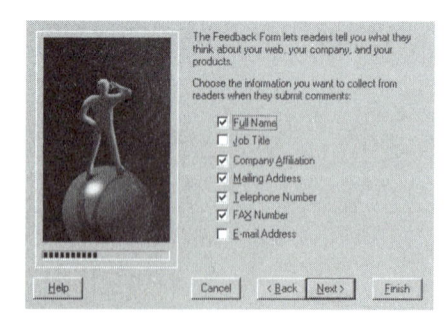

...contd

13 Here you customise how your Table of Contents is updated. Look in Help for advice on these settings.

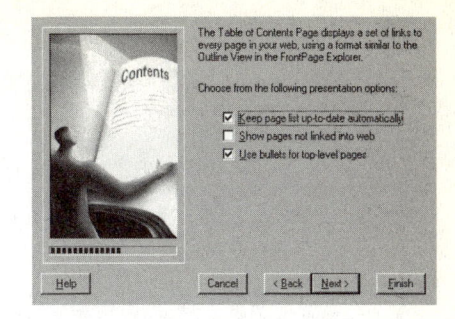

14 This is an important screen. Here you decide how the information from your customers will be formatted.

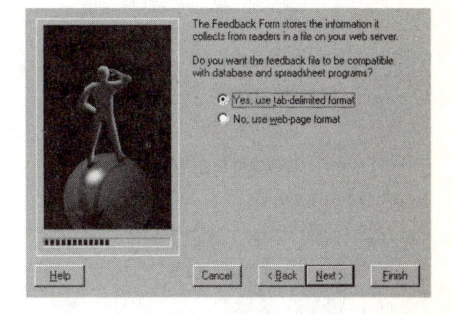

BEWARE

If you plan to use the information with a database such as Access, select the first option and the information will be stored in a format that you can use with this software.

15 Choose all the information that you want to appear at the bottom of each page.

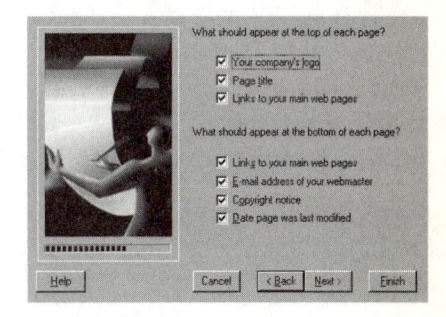

1. Getting Started **17**

...contd

16 The look and feel of your site are set here. Choose a style that reflects the character of your company.

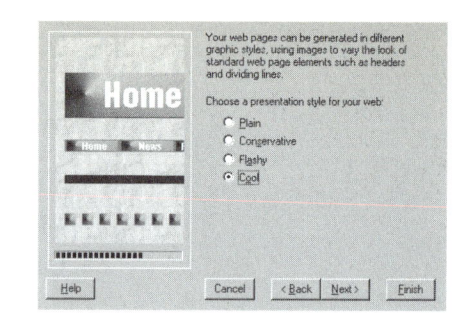

HANDY TIP

There is some debate about the use of under-construction icons. Some Webmasters feel that a site shouldn't go live until it is completely finished. You will have to make your own mind up about this.

17 Set the background and text colour for each page.

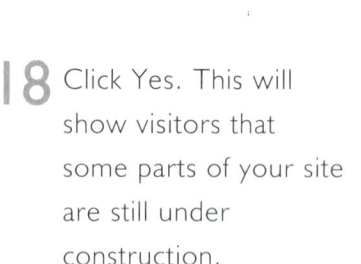

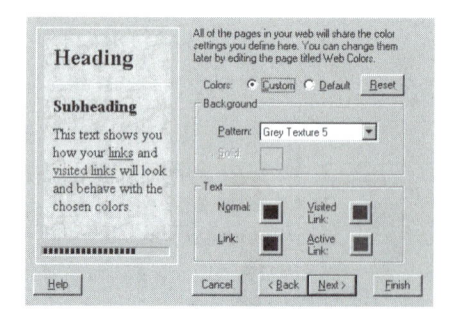

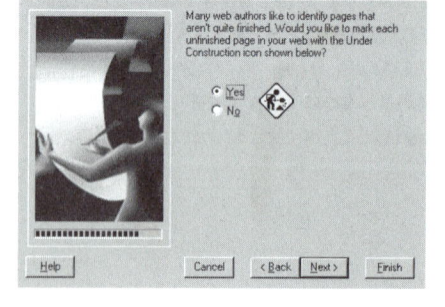

18 Click Yes. This will show visitors that some parts of your site are still under construction.

19 The following two screens offer huge time savings. Once this information is entered, it is included in each page of your Web site automatically.

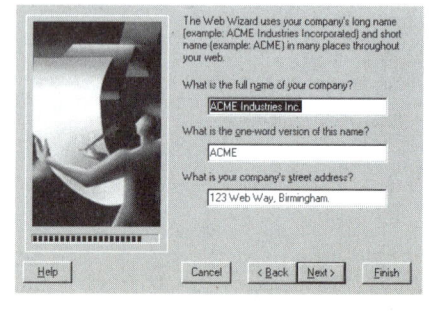

18   FrontPage in easy steps

...contd

20 This is the final screen of the Wizard. All the information will now be used to create the site. When this is done your new site will be opened into the Explorer ready for you to edit – as shown on the following page.

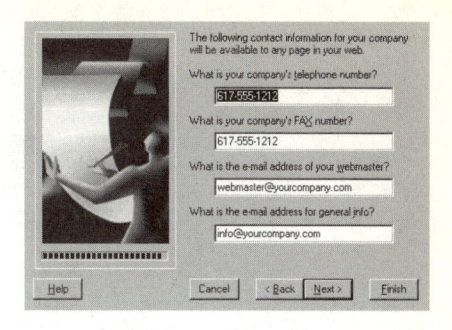

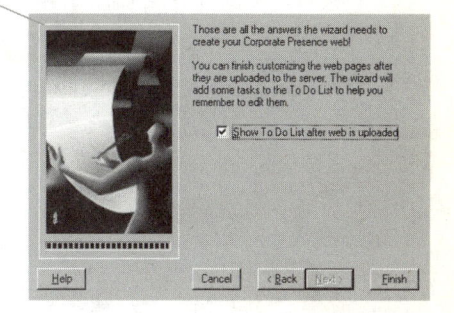

You have now completed all the screens in this Wizard. When you click on 'Finish', FrontPage will create all the pages of your Web site and include all the information that you typed in. This may take a few seconds. When this is done you will see the Web open in the Explorer and the Things To Do list will be displayed. This gives you a full list of the tasks that you need to complete before your Web is ready to go live.

1. Getting Started

...contd

This is the completed Web site opened in the Explorer. You will learn more about the Explorer in Chapter Two.

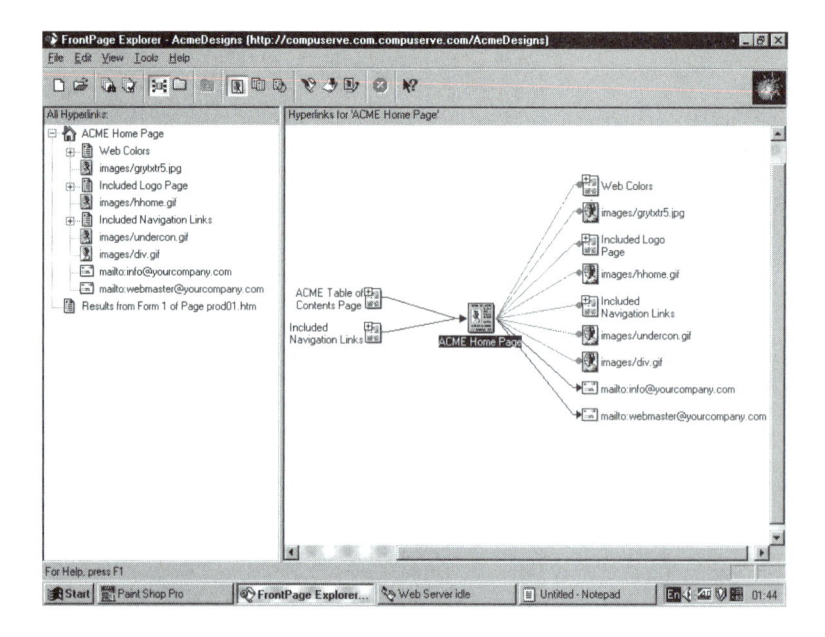

This is the process that you go through when you choose to use a Wizard to create a new Web. The dialogue box shown in step 3 on page 14 shows the wide variety that you have to choose from. You can of course combine Webs when they have been created to give you a unique Web site that you can customise before you publish it to your chosen server.

CHAPTER TWO

The Explorer

This chapter shows you how you can view your Web site and manipulate its various elements quickly and easily.

Covers

Viewing Your Site	22
Changing the View	25
Hyperlink View	27
Folder View	31
Importing Documents	33
Deleting a Web Site	34
Changing Web Settings	35
Changing Your Password	40
Verifying Your Links	41
Configuring Editors	42
Permissions	45

Viewing Your Site

When creating a new Web site, many designers have to resort to a very low-tech means of organising the hundreds of pages that can go up to make the site. Office walls become plastered with scraps of paper. FrontPage offers users a unique way of viewing their site. Changing the location of pages, adding or deleting pages becomes as easy as clicking your mouse.

1   Click Start, then Programs, and click on the FrontPage entry as it pops up. Or click on the FrontPage icon that you have dragged onto the desktop as a shortcut.

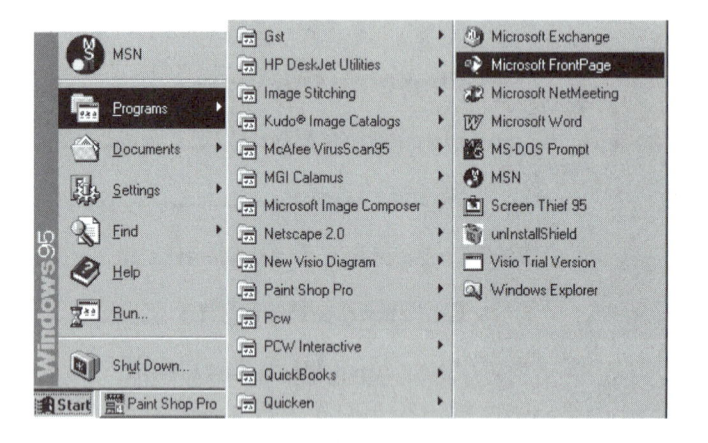

2   The FrontPage Explorer opens. It is blank, as you have not loaded a Web site yet. You will see the dialogue box that is explained on page 13 open for you to choose a Web.

FrontPage in easy steps

...contd

3 This is the main toolbar of the Explorer:

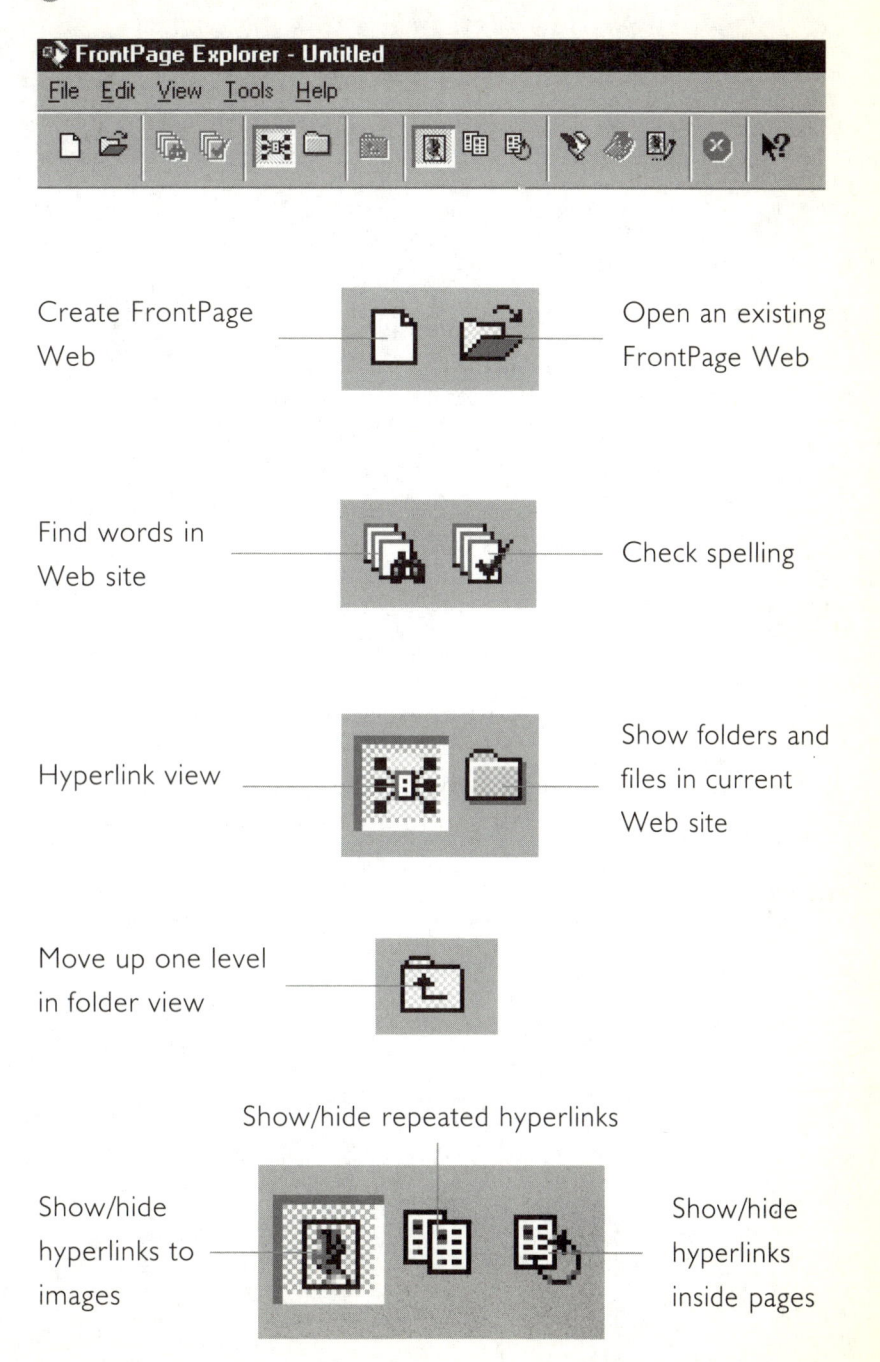

Create FrontPage Web — Open an existing FrontPage Web

Find words in Web site — Check spelling

Hyperlink view — Show folders and files in current Web site

Move up one level in folder view

Show/hide repeated hyperlinks

Show/hide hyperlinks to images — Show/hide hyperlinks inside pages

2. The Explorer **23**

...contd

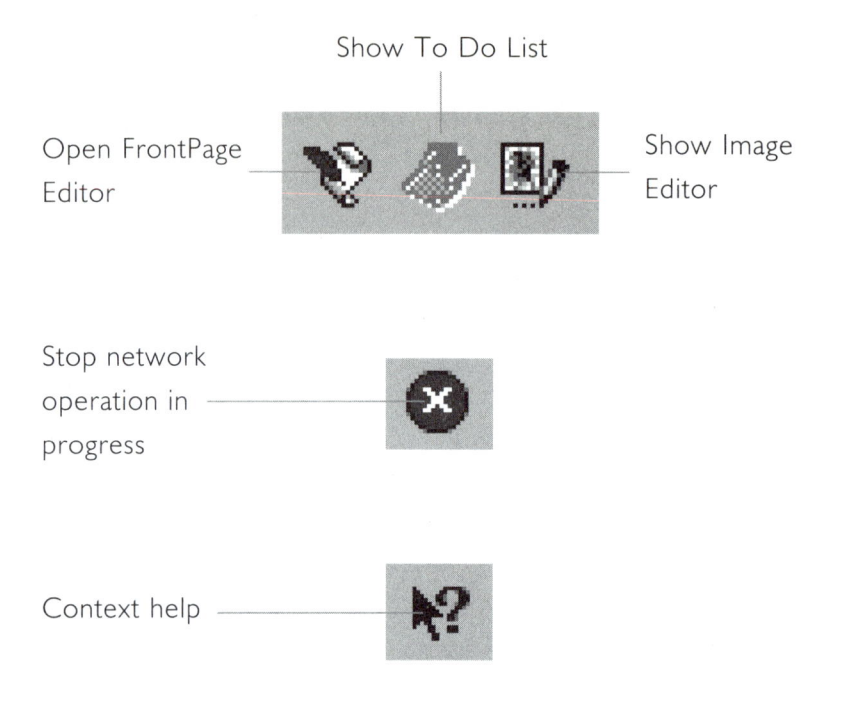

Open FrontPage Editor — Show To Do List — Show Image Editor

Stop network operation in progress

Context help

With these icons you have complete control over which Web you have in the Explorer and how it is displayed. This gives you a clear picture of the pages that you have on your site and how they relate to each other.

Changing the View

The power of the Explorer is its ability to show you what your Web site looks like in a number of different formats. Explorer is also the place that you usually create new Web sites. Clicking on the New Site icon will activate the New Web Wizard. You have already seen this in action in the last chapter.

1. Click on this icon from the toolbar at the top of the Explorer screen.

2. This dialogue box will appear:

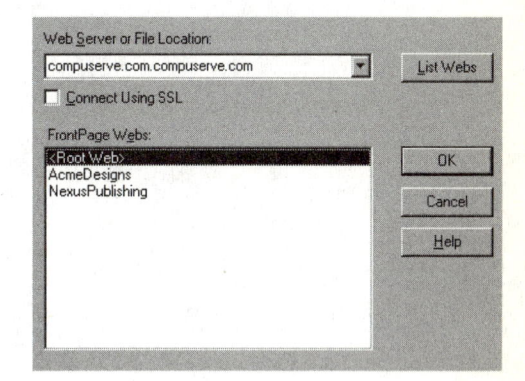

3. Click the 'List Webs' button. In the large window you will see a list of all the Web sites you have created.

4. Double-click on the Web site you want to open. FrontPage will open the Web and display its contents in the Explorer, as you see on the next page.

2. The Explorer

...contd

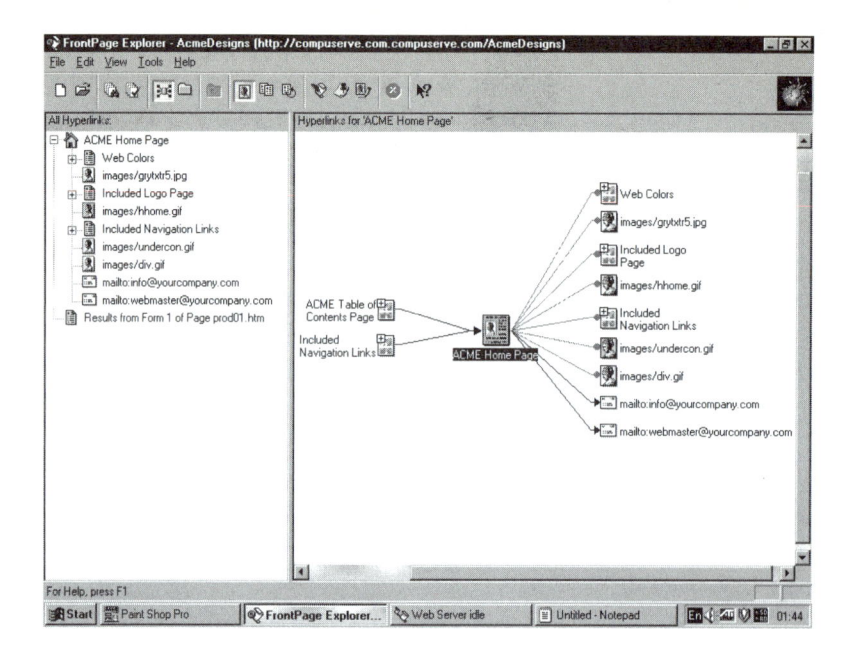

This is the FrontPage Explorer as you will see it when you open any Web site that you have created. As you can see, its main window is split into two. The left should be familiar to Windows users: the Windows Explorer uses a similar layout of files and folders. The right side of the screen gives FrontPage its power. You can view your site, or any part of it, and the links that each page has to them and away from them to other areas of the Web site.

Hyperlink View

The left side of the screen is very similar to the Explorer in Windows. Clicking on the plus signs will open the next folder down in the tree. Do this now with one of the files. You will see that the display on the right changes with each mouse click. The FrontPage Explorer keeps track of your clicks and updates the hyperlinks to each page on your site.

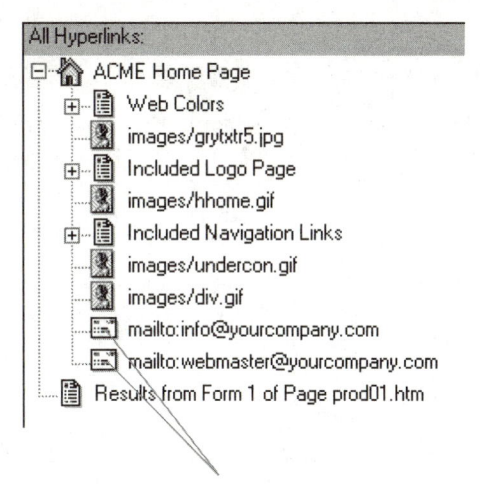

```
All Hyperlinks:
⊟─🏠 ACME Home Page
   ⊞─📄 Web Colors
   │   🖼 images/grytxtr5.jpg
   ⊞─📄 Included Logo Page
   │   🖼 images/hhome.gif
   ⊞─📄 Included Navigation Links
   │   🖼 images/undercon.gif
   │   🖼 images/div.gif
   │   ✉ mailto:info@yourcompany.com
   │   ✉ mailto:webmaster@yourcompany.com
   └─📄 Results from Form 1 of Page prod01.htm
```

These are the mail icons. They indicate that your visitors can send you e-mail from these pages.

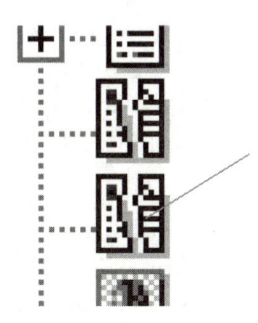

Watch carefully for these icons, as they indicate a broken link. You must fix all broken links before you publish your Web site, or it will not operate correctly.

2. The Explorer

...contd

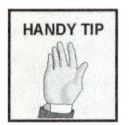

HANDY TIP

To centre a page on your screen, right-click on the file and choose 'Move to Centre' from the pop-up menu.

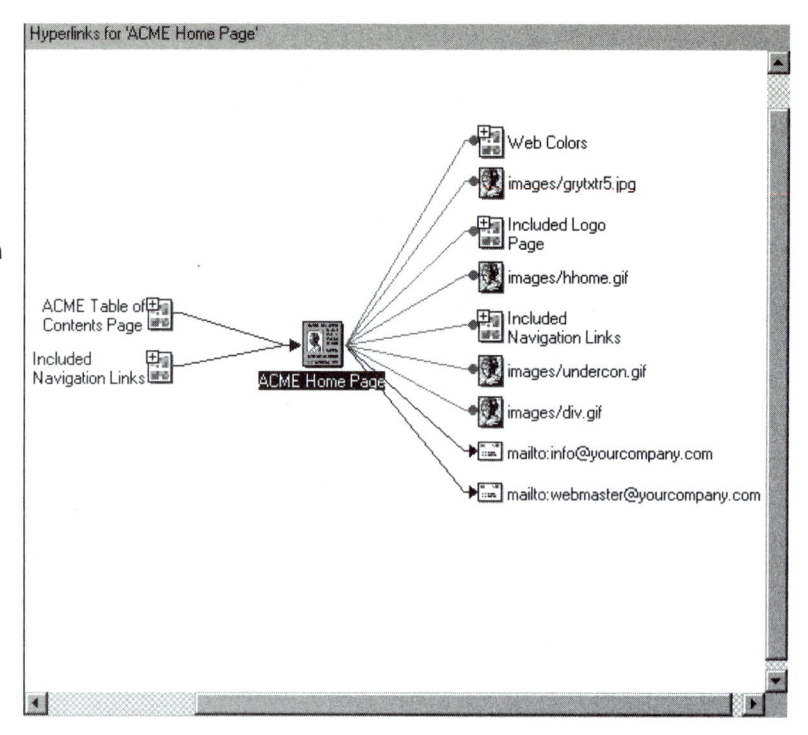

The right side of the screen is the main window in Hyperlink View, as you can see above. This is where you can really see the power and versatility of FrontPage when in Hyperlink mode. Here, all of your site is accessible. All the major elements are shown when you first open the site. You can move around the site by simply clicking on one of the pages here. Any modifications to a page can be done by double-clicking on the page. This automatically launches the FrontPage Editor.

Try clicking on a few pages now. You will notice that clicking on a page does not alter the file tree on the left of the screen. You have to click manually on a file in this section if you wish to view it in the main window.

...contd

Indicates an image file

Web Colors

images/grytxtr5.jpg

Included Logo Page

images/hhome.gif

Included Navigation Links

images/undercon.gif

images/div.gif

mailto:info@yourcomp

mailto:webmaster@you

Indicates the file on the right is included in the file on the left. Here for instance the image file is linked to the homepage, as this is where it appears.

Indicates a link to another item

Indicates mail can be sent from this page

2. The Explorer   **29**

...contd

Web Colors

images/grytxtr5.jpg

Included Logo Page

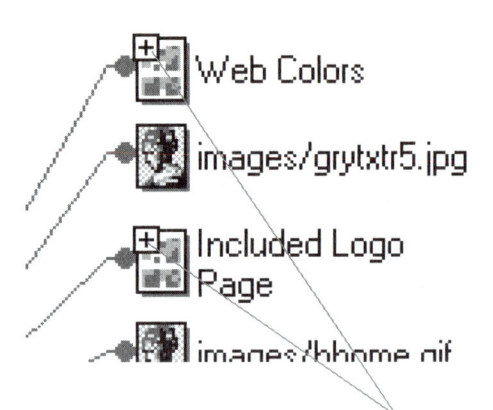

images/bhome.gif

Clicking on these plus signs will take you to the next set of pages that link to this page.

Hyperlink View offers you the best means of visualising your site. As it becomes more and more complex as you add pages and links, the number of pages that you can see at one time is dictated by the size of your monitor. The window can be resized, and the whole view can be moved either with the scroll bars or by clicking on some empty space in the window. Your mouse pointer will then change to a hand, indicating that you can move the view in the window with your mouse.

Folder View

Sometimes called summary view, this shows the web you have opened as a complete list of all the files it contains. As with Hyperlink View, the left of the screen can be clicked on to change the files that are viewable in the main window on the right. This is a fast way of locating a file whose location you are not sure of. Searching for it in Hyperlink View would be time-consuming.

HANDY TIP **As with Hyperlink View, if you double-click on a file in this mode it will be opened in its associated editor.**

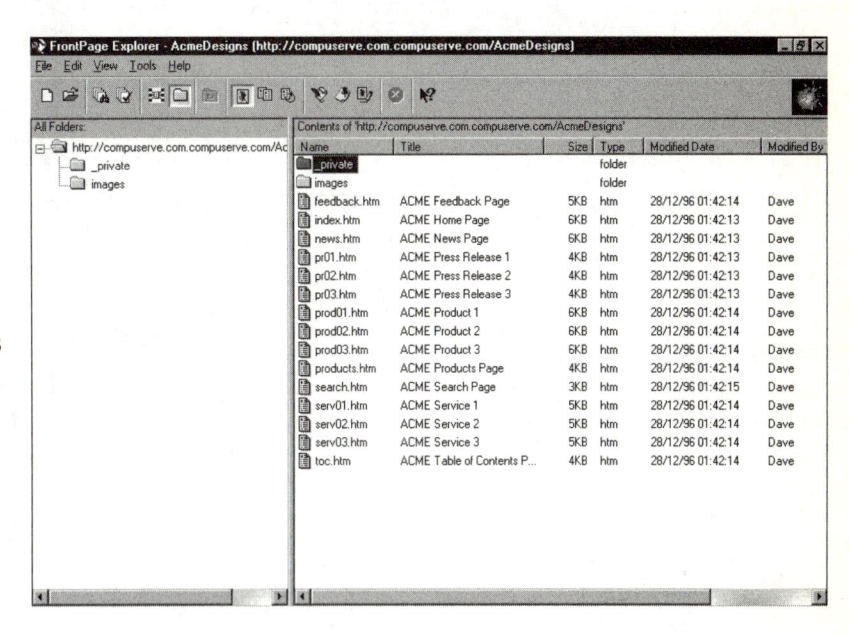

These are the two main icons in this viewing mode.

HTML file   Image file

2. The Explorer

31

...contd

If you forget what a file is, or when you created it, you can refer to the index that FrontPage keeps of all the files that you create.

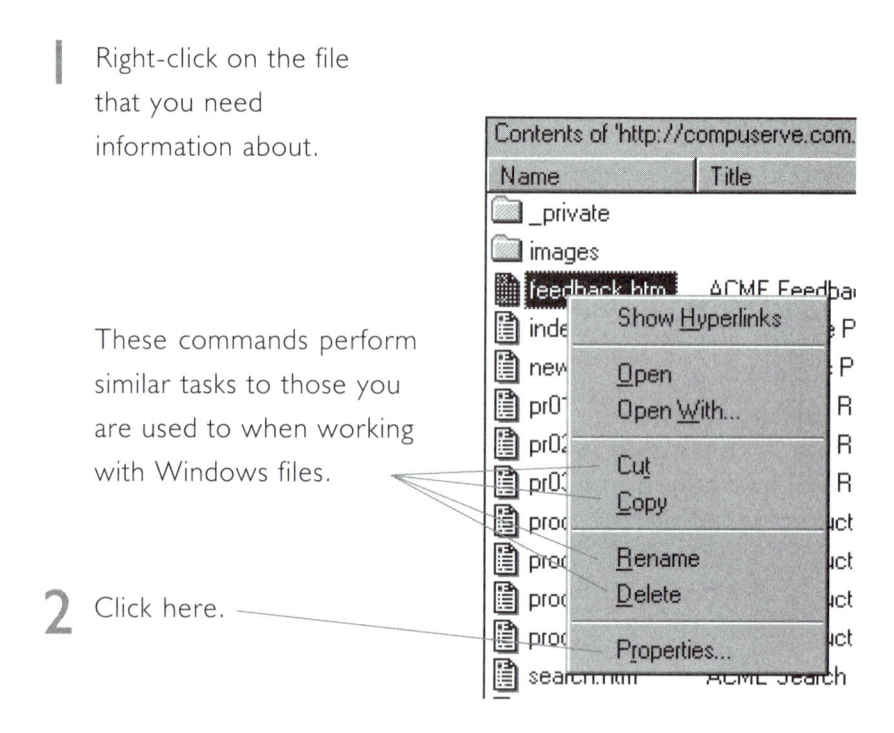

1 Right-click on the file that you need information about.

These commands perform similar tasks to those you are used to when working with Windows files.

2 Click here.

3 This is the main Properties dialogue box.

Click here to discover who created the file, when it was modified and by whom, and any comments the designer left.

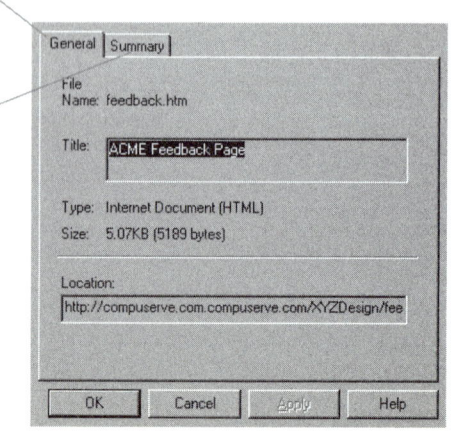

32 **FrontPage in easy steps**

Importing Documents

You can add documents that you created in other programs to FrontPage without any problems.

HANDY TIP — **When you have clicked the Import button, it will change to a Stop button. You can stop the import process at any time by clicking on this.**

1. Choose Import from the File menu. This dialogue box will open.

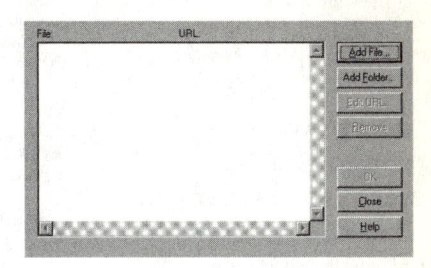

2. Click on 'Add File'. This will open the usual Windows file selector.

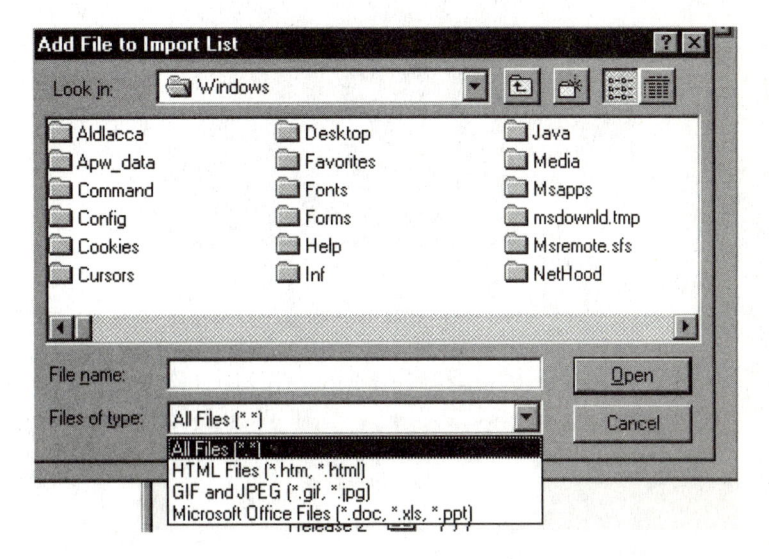

3. Choose the file or files you want to import. They will be imported and added to the bottom of the Hyperlink View.

2. The Explorer

Deleting a Web Site

Make sure you definitely want to delete the site. It cannot be recovered when you have completed this operation, even from the Windows Recycle Bin!

There may be a time when you want to delete a site from your server. You must choose the Delete Web command from the File menu. Do not remove the files manually from your server, as FrontPage may not recognise what you have done. This could affect your remaining sites.

When you have clicked on this menu item, you will see the familiar warning dialogue box pop up. This is the only chance you have to change your mind. If you click 'OK', the Web site will be deleted permanently.

Changing Web Settings

Parameters

You can change common elements that appear throughout your site with the least amount of work. If your E-mail address changes, for instance, using other programs you would face the task of manually changing the address on hundreds of pages in some cases. With FrontPage you can do this with the click of a mouse. You can open this dialogue box through the 'Tools' menu.

1 Choose Web Settings from the Tools menu.

2 In the dialogue box that opens, highlight one of the entries in the window by clicking on it with your mouse – in this case, highlight the company address.

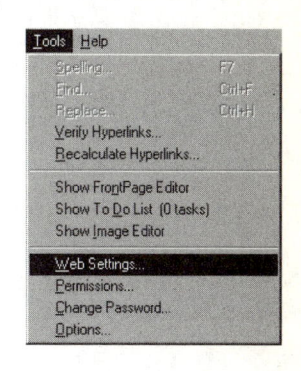

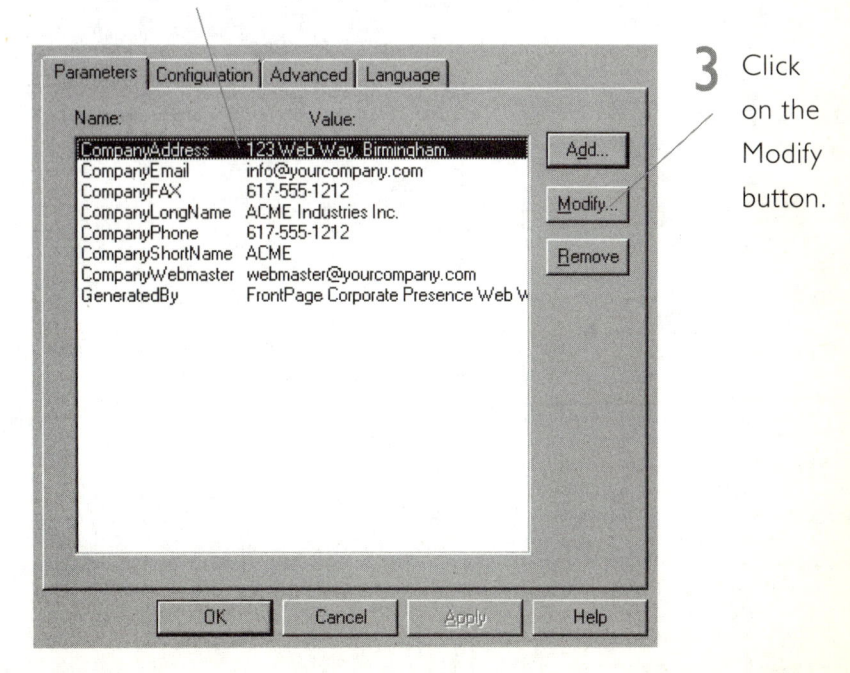

3 Click on the Modify button.

2. The Explorer

35

...contd

4   This dialogue will pop up. You can modify the information in the windows.

   | Name: | CompanyAddress |
   | Value: | 123 Albert Road, Manchester, WS9 7AP. |

   OK   Cancel   Help

5   Similarly, if you click on the Add button (see page 35) you can add to the list of Web settings that appears in the first screen.

   Name:
   Value:

   OK   Cancel   Help

36   FrontPage in easy steps

...contd

Configuration
Use this tab to view the Web settings of the current Web you have open.

This is the name of the current Web. If you are the Web Administrator authorised in the root web, you can change this name by typing it here.

This is the name of the Web as it appears in the title bar of the Explorer. This is usually a descriptive name; it must start with a letter and can have up to 31 characters.

This is the URL of the Web server.

Shown here is the version number of the programs installed on your server that manage FrontPage.

The IP (Internet Protocol) address of your server. These are like telephone numbers. Each computer is assigned a unique number to identify it. Your Internet service provider will give you this number.

This is the URL of the Proxy server. This is the server that acts as a filter between your computer server and the Internet.

2. The Explorer

37

...contd

Advanced
Here you set advanced features that can be attached to your current Web.

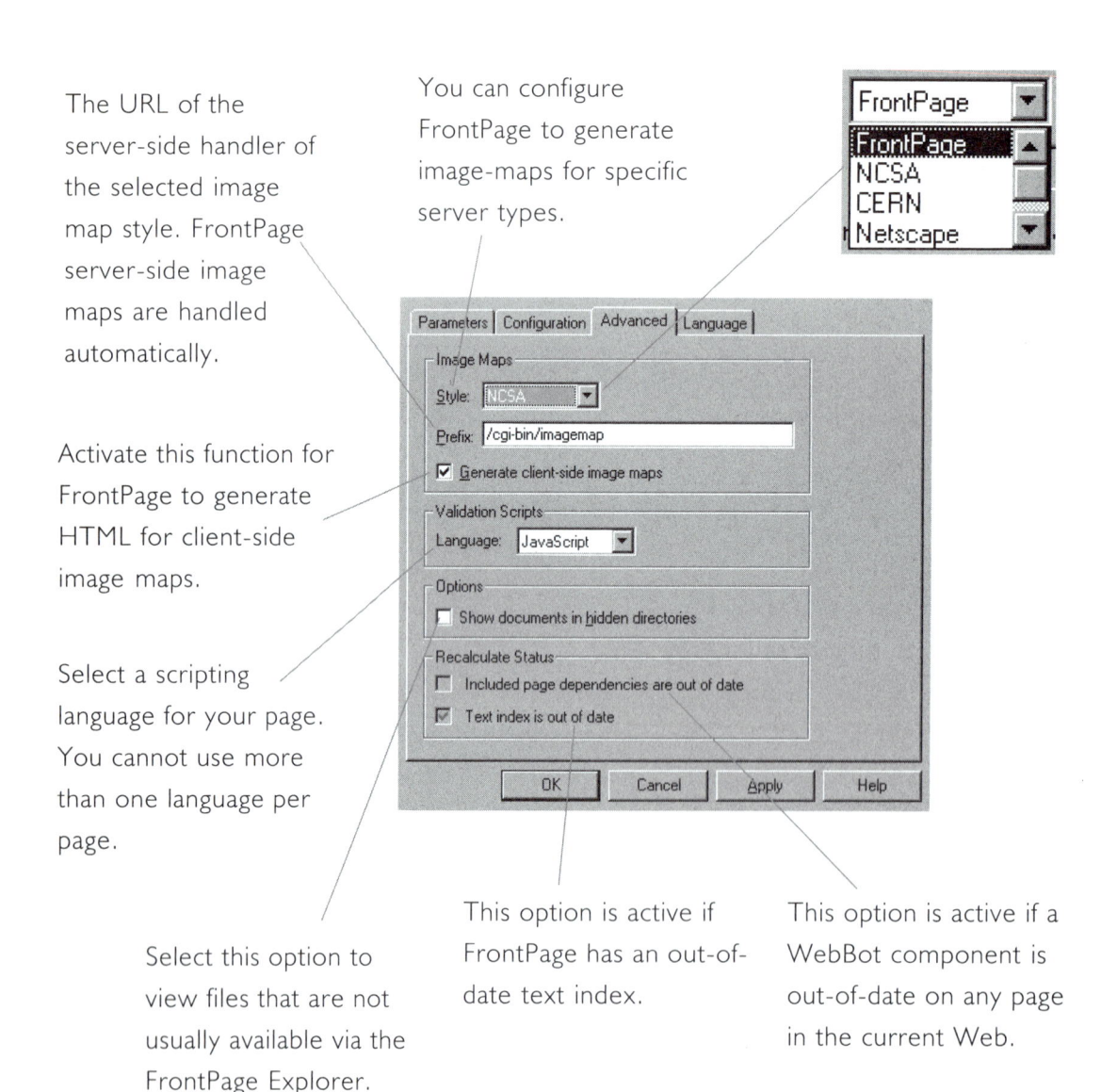

The URL of the server-side handler of the selected image map style. FrontPage server-side image maps are handled automatically.

You can configure FrontPage to generate image-maps for specific server types.

Activate this function for FrontPage to generate HTML for client-side image maps.

Select a scripting language for your page. You cannot use more than one language per page.

Select this option to view files that are not usually available via the FrontPage Explorer.

This option is active if FrontPage has an out-of-date text index.

This option is active if a WebBot component is out-of-date on any page in the current Web.

38 FrontPage in easy steps

...contd

Language
Use the settings in this tab to change the FrontPage Web language or HTML coding.

This option sets the language that will be used to return any error messages from the server when using the FrontPage Server Extensions. If you are creating a Web site in another language, change this setting so that the language of the messages coming from the server matches the language used in your Web site.

If you want your Web pages to be saved in a different character set than that which is set up on your computer, select the character set from the drop-down list. Any new pages will be saved with this character set by default.

2. The Explorer

Changing Your Password

There may come a time when you need to change your password. The password that you set when you first set up your site can be changed as many times as you like. But, as before, you must make sure that you type it exactly each time, paying special attention to the upper- and lower-case letters that you use. Open this dialogue through the Tools menu.

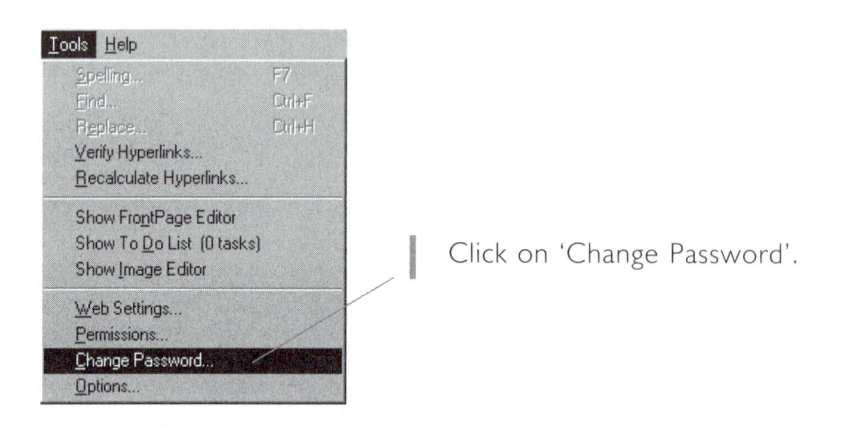

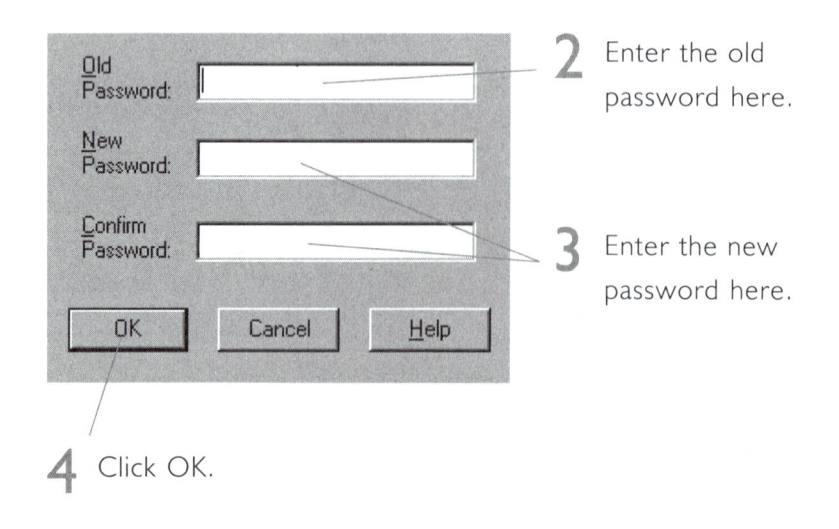

1 Click on 'Change Password'.

2 Enter the old password here.

3 Enter the new password here.

4 Click OK.

Verifying Your Links

Links are what make your Web site work. Each time a visitor clicks on a link, they expect to be taken to the next page on your site. It's your responsibility to make sure that all pages link to the next one.

As always, FrontPage does most of the work for you, in that it looks at your site, lists all the broken links, and lets you know if they are internal or external. This dialogue can be opened by selecting 'Verify Hyperlinks' from the Tools menu.

REMEMBER **The links that are listed in the Verify dialogue only tell you that the link exists. It does not confirm that it links to the page it is supposed to.**

HANDY TIP **The best way to check links is to try and browse the site with a Web browser. This will show up any broken links instantly.**

Yellow indicates that the link has been edited.

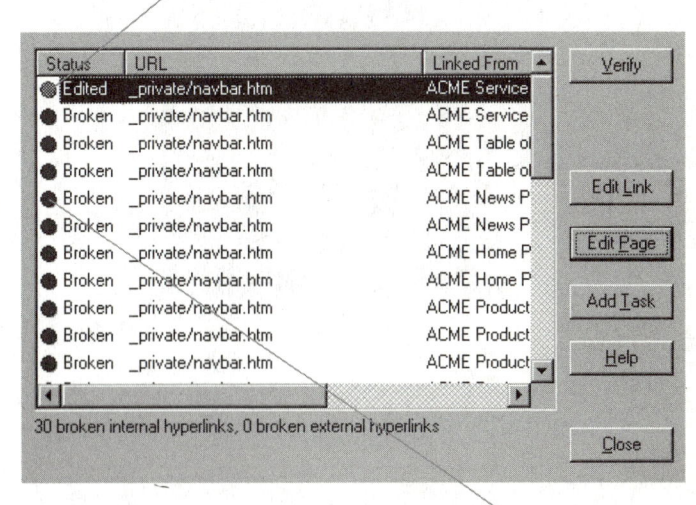

Green indicates that the link exists.

Red indicates that the link is broken.

2. The Explorer

41

Configuring Editors

As you verify links, FrontPage has the ability to link a specific file format to an editor of your choice. For instance, if you are using a large number of graphics on a page, and want to edit them, you can tell FrontPage to use your favourite graphics program to edit the graphics. This also goes for any file format that you have on your Web site.

1 From the Tools menu in the Explorer, choose Options.

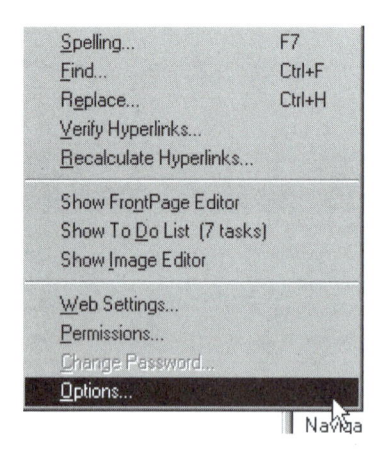

2 This dialogue box will open. Click on the Configure Editors tab.

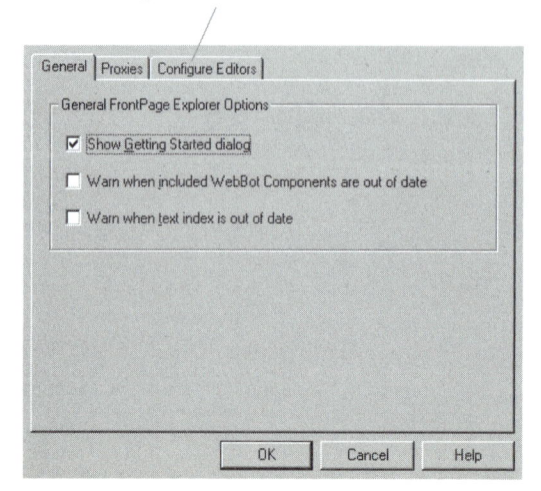

FrontPage in easy steps

...contd

3 You can see in this window that the graphic files on the Web site have been linked to Image Composer, which comes on the FrontPage CD-ROM. If you want to link these files to another graphics program, you can do so by clicking on the Add button. Do this now.

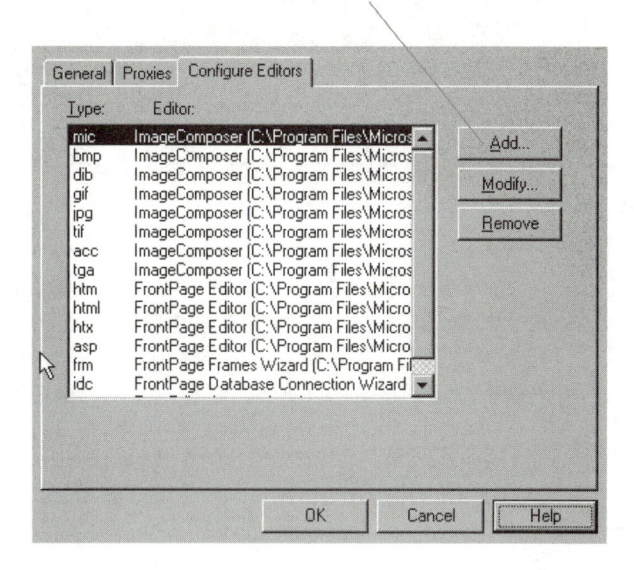

4 In this dialogue box you can choose the type of file that you want to link an editor to, the editor name and the path to the editor on your hard drive. If you don't know this, click on 'Browse' and locate it in the usual way.

2. The Explorer **43**

...contd

5 Use the Modify button to modify an existing editor configuration:

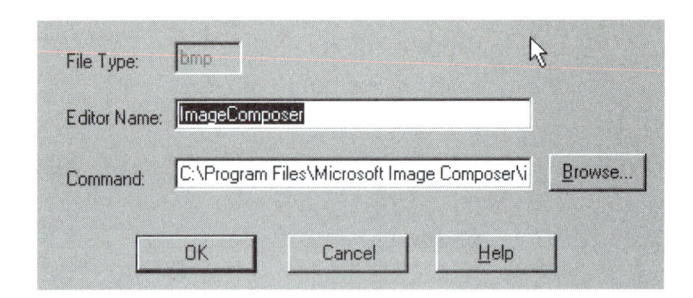

File Type:	bmp
Editor Name:	ImageComposer
Command:	C:\Program Files\Microsoft Image Composer\i

You have now linked your files to specific editors. Each time you want to edit a file – for instance a text file – FrontPage will know which editor you prefer to use and open this. As you can see from the dialogue box at the top of this page, you can change these settings when you wish. If you find a new editor you want to use, you can link all the files to it that used to link to the old editor. This is true for all file formats.

Permissions

Your Web site's security should be taken as seriously as the security you have for other parts of your business. Via the Explorer you can set who has access to the Web pages on one or more of the Web sites that you build with FrontPage. To make the changes below, you must have Administrator access to the Web site you are working on. If you don't, then you probably shouldn't be doing this anyway!

1 Open the FrontPage Web you would like to work on in the Explorer, then go to the Tools menu and click on 'Permissions'.

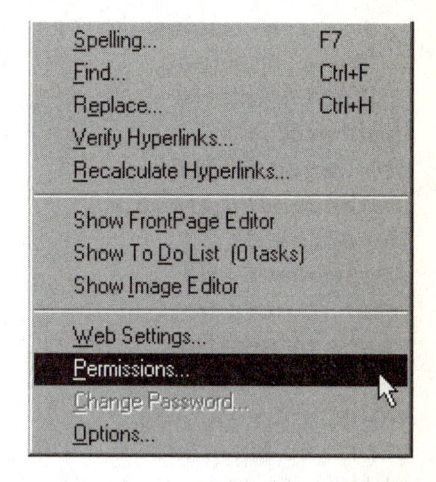

2 From this dialogue box you set the access privileges for any of the Webs you have built.

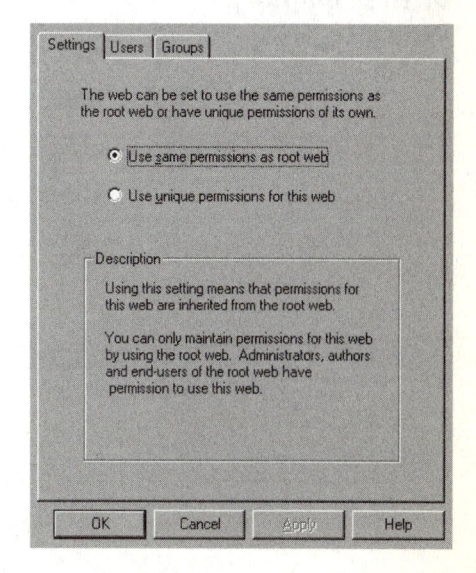

2. The Explorer

...contd

HANDY TIP

Don't be too hasty to decide that you will not want to limit access privileges. If, for instance, you are in the accounts department and want to keep next year's projections to yourself for a while, you can limit access to this part of the company Web site.

3 Click on the Users tab to open this dialogue box. From here you can set who has access to which sites and also what level of access they have.

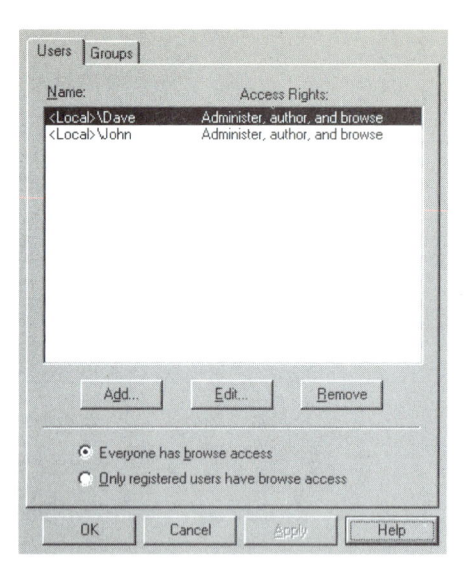

4 If you want to edit the list of users who have access to a particular Web site, click on the 'Edit' button. This dialogue will come up for you to enter the information.

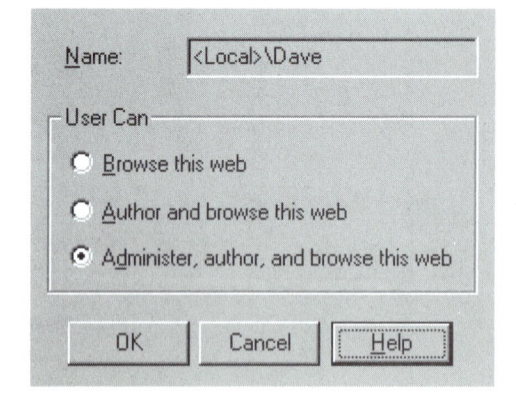

FrontPage in easy steps

...contd

5 If you have a new user to whom you want to give access to your Web site you can do so through the Add Users dialogue box. As you can see, you can give the user any level of privilege you like.

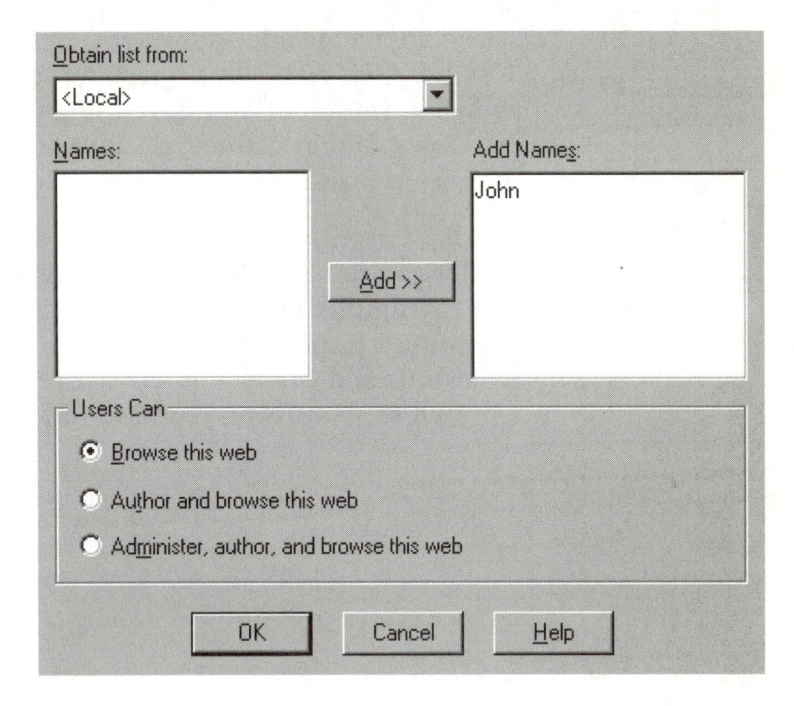

Access to a Web site is usually split into three levels of privilege:

Administrator

This is the most superior user of the Web. They have full access to the Web that is currently in the Explorer and all other Webs on the network. They have the power to delete entire Webs as well as create new ones. They are also the people who assign Web access privileges to the other users on the network who will be accessing the site.

...contd

Author
Even though they are authors, they do not have the access to delete the whole Web. They can delete pages, edit and create new ones.

End User
These are the people who view your site through a standard Web browser, either over the Internet itself, or via your company Intranet. They have the most limited access privileges as they cannot in any way modify the Web pages they are viewing.

You have even further control over the access that you give to those working on or using your Web site, through the Server Administrator. This is covered in more detail on pages 142-144 in Chapter Eight. From there you can assign passwords and change old ones if you think there has been a breach of security or you have forgotten it.

CHAPTER THREE

The Editor

This chapter will show you the FrontPage Editor. Here you take the Web pages that you have created with a Wizard and add text and graphics to make your site unique.

Covers

Starting the Editor	50
The Toolbar	51
Tables	54
Comments	57
Marquee Tags	58
HTML Commands	61
The To Do List	64
Frames	67
Creating a Custom Frame	70
Text Files	73

Starting the Editor

The Editor is opened from the Explorer. You can either double-click on a page in Hyperlink View, or on a file in Folder View. You can also call the Editor up any time with the icon in the toolbar of the Explorer.

In the toolbar, click on the 'Open Editor' icon as shown below:

Open Editor icon

This is the Editor's main window. From here you load in your pages and add text and graphics to create your finished page:

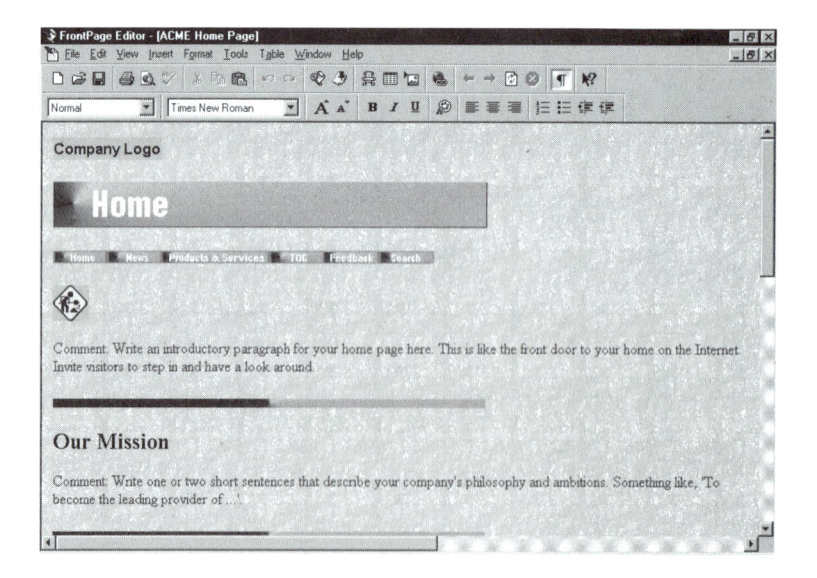

The Toolbar

This is the main toolbar, with all of the basic function icons visible:

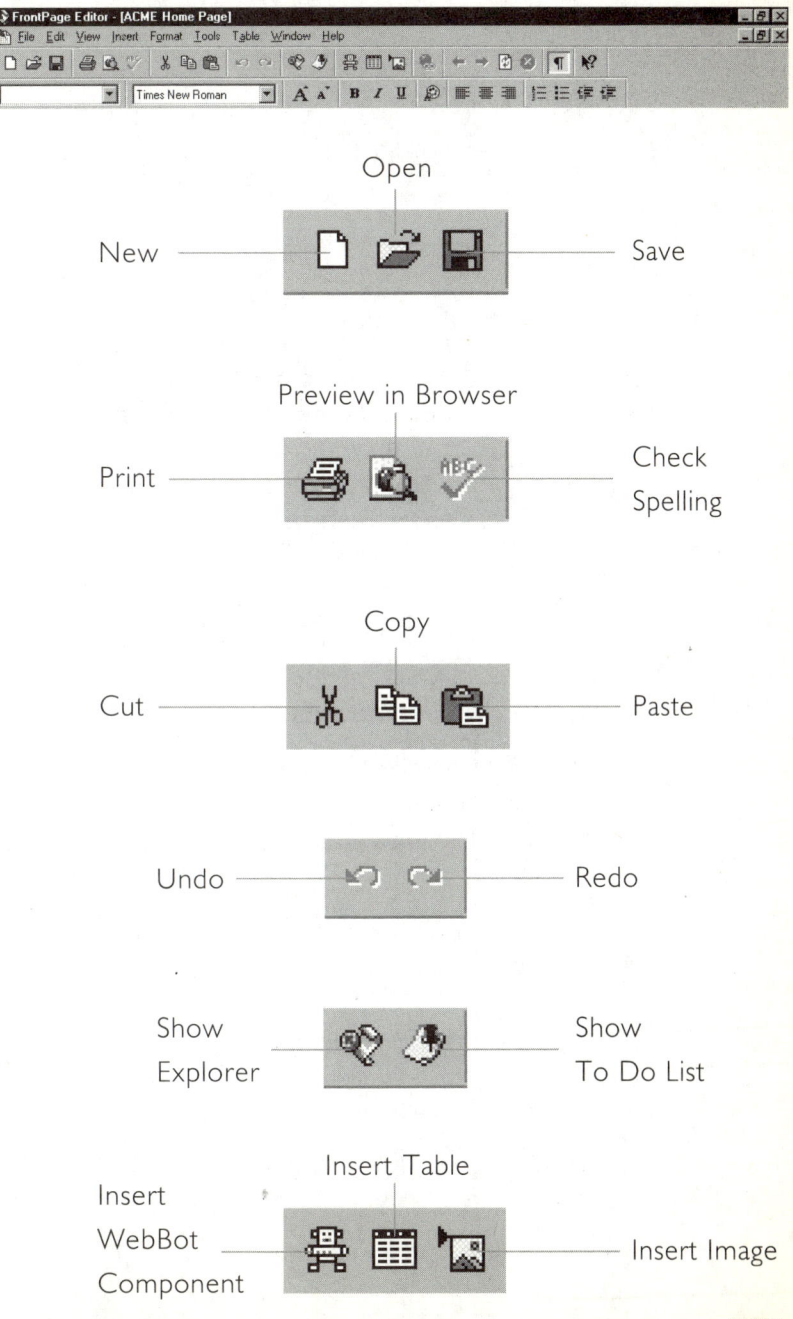

New — Open — Save

Print — Preview in Browser — Check Spelling

Cut — Copy — Paste

Undo — Redo

Show Explorer — Show To Do List

Insert WebBot Component — Insert Table — Insert Image

3. The Editor

...contd

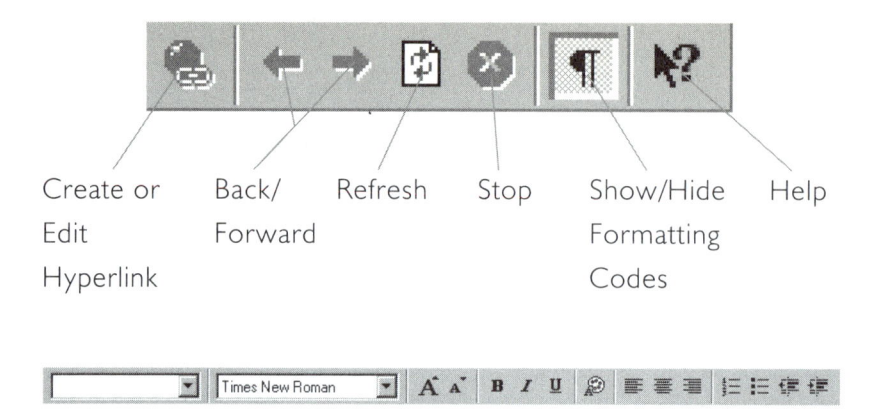

Create or Edit Hyperlink | Back/Forward | Refresh | Stop | Show/Hide Formatting Codes | Help

This set of icons should be familiar as they follow the usual conventions for most word-processors. The text that you enter into the window in the Editor can be formatted in the same way as you would format the text if you were writing a letter in your favourite word-processor. Below you can see a page open in the Editor, showing some of the effects that you can apply to the text you enter.

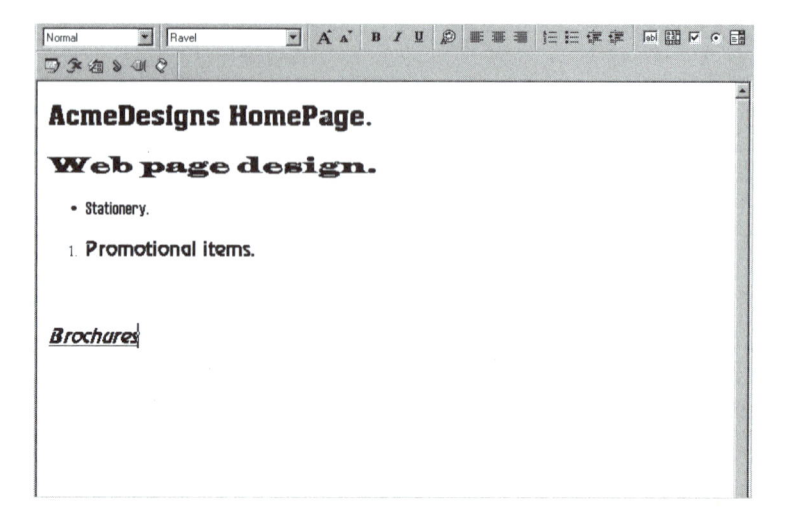

AcmeDesigns HomePage.

Web page design.

- Stationery.
1. Promotional items.

Brochures

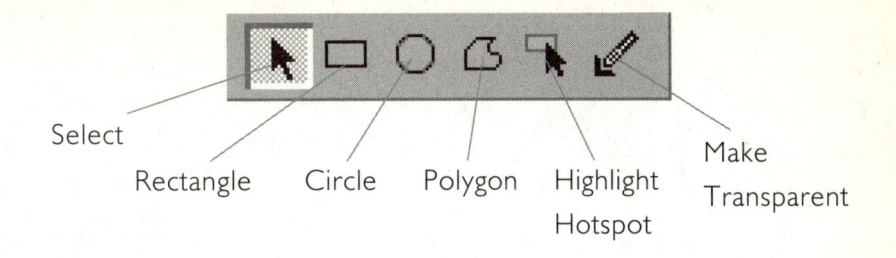

...contd

Select — Rectangle — Circle — Polygon — Highlight Hotspot — Make Transparent

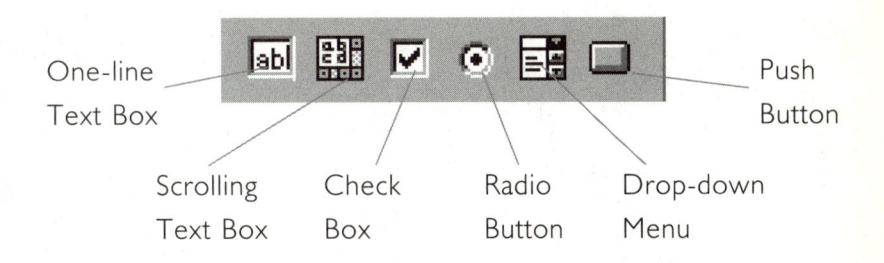

One-line Text Box — Scrolling Text Box — Check Box — Radio Button — Drop-down Menu — Push Button

BEWARE

Before using these icons you should understand the consequences of their advanced features.

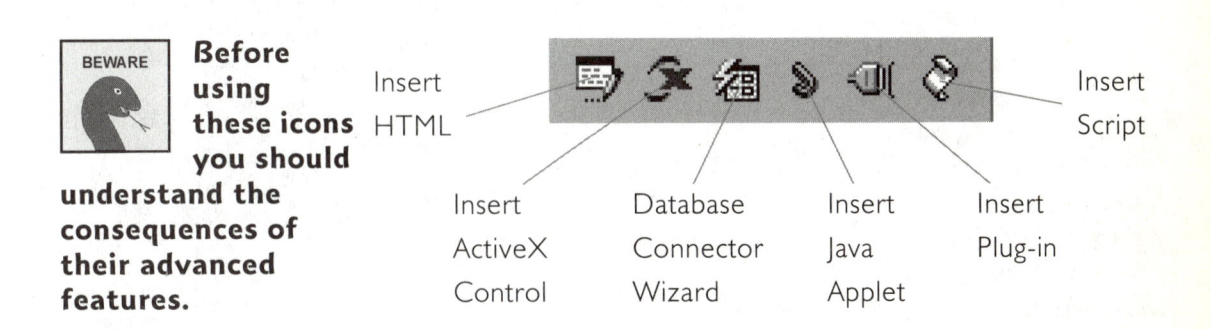

Insert HTML — Insert ActiveX Control — Database Connector Wizard — Insert Java Applet — Insert Plug-in — Insert Script

3. The Editor 53

Tables

Tables are one of the most useful sorts of elements that you can put onto your Web pages. They can contain any kind of information you want. The FrontPage Editor offers the user an easy way of creating and modifying tables.

1 Click on the Table menu, and then on the 'Insert table' entry in the menu.

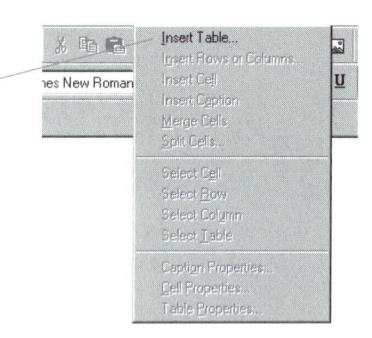

2 In this dialogue box, define the layout of your table, then click OK.

REMEMBER

The browser that your table will be viewed in will determine greatly how your table will look when it is viewed on your Web site.

If you want a border around your table, enter the value in pixels here. If not, enter a value of 0.

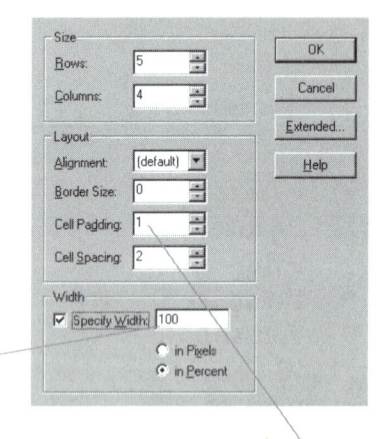

Cell padding is the space between the contents of the cell and the cell's borders.

54   **FrontPage in easy steps**

...contd

3 Once you've clicked OK in the previous dialogue, the Editor will display the table you have just defined:

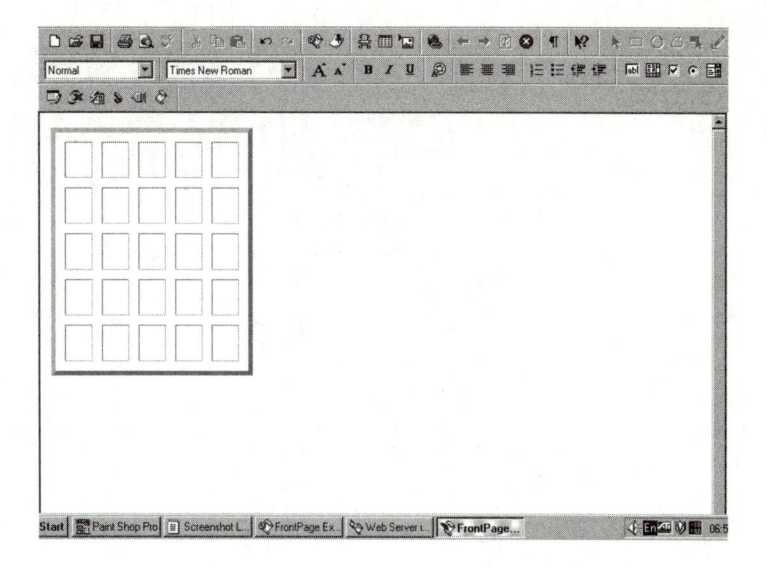

4 If you open the Table menu again, you can see that you have a number of options for manipulating the look and layout of your table. Click on 'Cell Properties'.

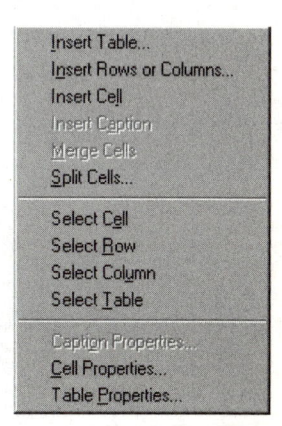

3. The Editor

...contd

5 With the Cell Properties dialogue box you have complete control over the appearance and layout of the cells contained within each table.

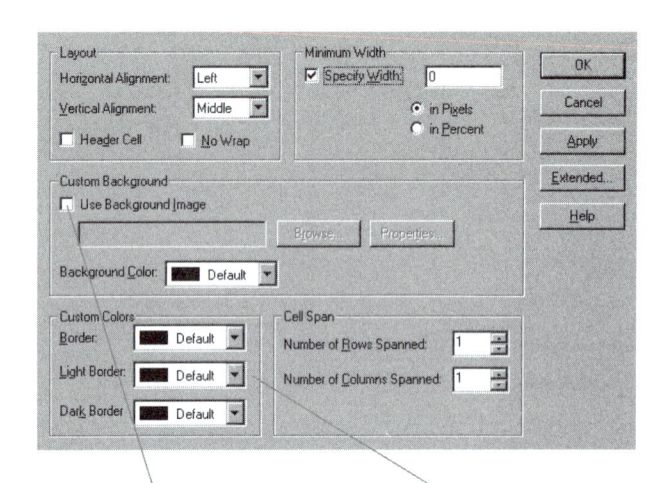

You can select an image or colour for the cell with this option. The image can be completely different from the page image.

You have complete control over the colours you can choose for the table and cell borders.

5 The Table Properties dialogue box uses many of the same parameters to govern the appearance of the table as a whole.

Comments

As you create your Web pages you will want to make notes as you go. There's nothing worse than a desk full of scrap paper with these notes scribbled on them. In FrontPage you can leave yourself a note right on the page you are working on. You will always see it – until you delete, it of course – and it won't get lost or forgotten.

1 From the Editor, open the Insert menu and click on the Comment entry.

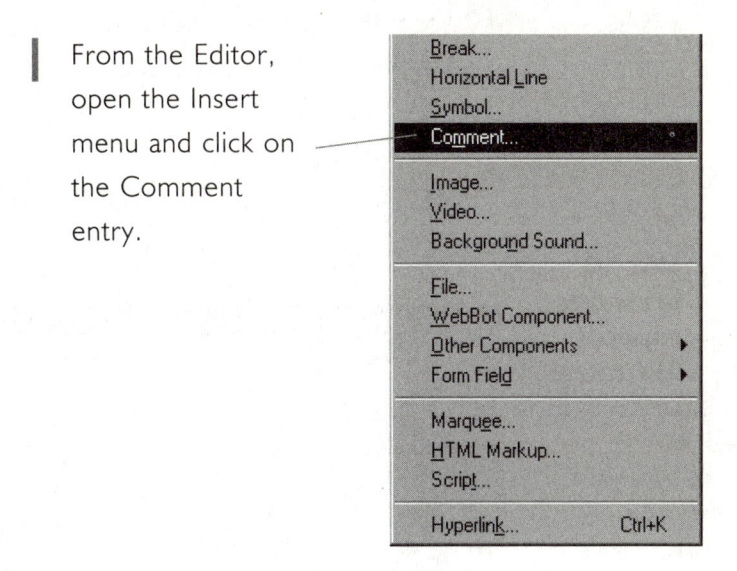

2 You will see this dialogue open. You can now enter whatever notes you want to leave yourself and place them on the page at the cursor point. They are invisible when the page is viewed with a browser, even when connected to the Internet.

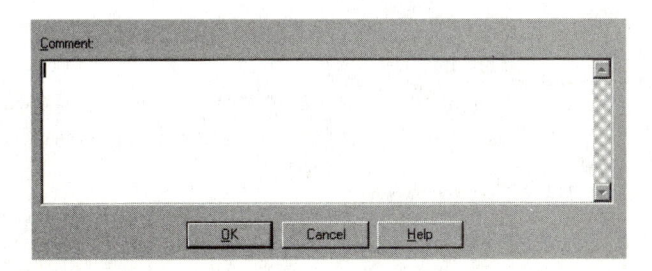

3. The Editor 57

Marquee Tags

You may well have seen this feature on some of the Web sites that you have accessed, but didn't know what it was called. Some sites have text that scrolls across the screen. It allows the site designer to draw attention to the text he wants you to click on, or to give you an essential message.

1 From the Editor, open the Insert menu and click on the Marquee entry.

2 This dialogue box will open. You set all of the Marquee's settings from here. To view the finished Marquee choose Preview in Browser from the File menu.

REMEMBER **Not all browsers support Marquees. In this case normal text will be inserted, but you won't see the animation.**

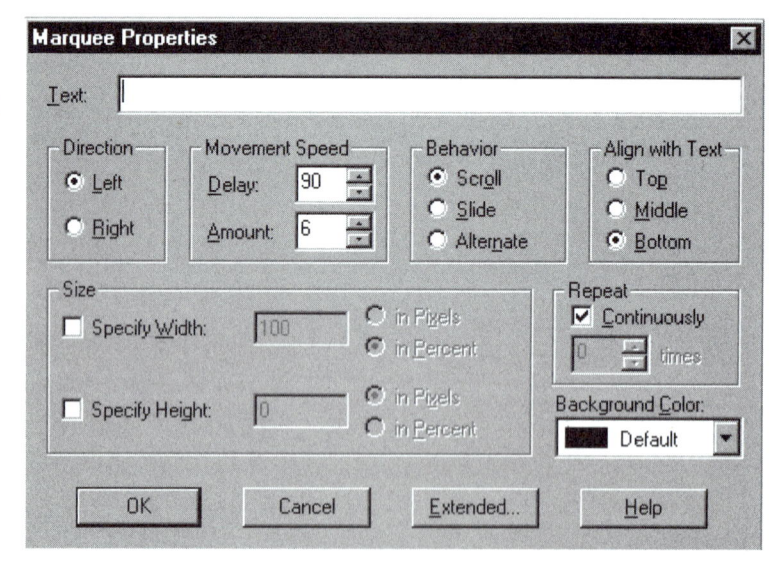

Text
Enter the text you would like animated. If it is already on the page, select it and it will appear in this window.

Direction
Choose the direction that you want the text to move in.

58 FrontPage in easy steps

...contd

Movement Speed
Choose how fast you would like the text to move.

Delay
Set how long a delay you would like before the text will move when the page is viewed.

Amount
This determines how much the text will move across your screen. This is in pixels.

Behaviour
Choose the type of motion your text should have.

Scroll
Sets the text to scroll continuously across the screen in the direction you specified.

Slide
This causes the text to slide into the browser window, move across the screen to the opposite border and stop.

Alternate
A variation on Slide. Here the text moves back and forth from border to border.

Align With Text
Specify how the Marquee text is to align with the normal text on your page.

Size
Usually the size of a Marquee is governed by the size of the text. You can set the space that the Marquee takes up manually here.

Specify Width/Height
Here you can specify the exact width of the Marquee region. You can enter a value as pixels or as a percentage. Pixels will define the rectangle of the Marquee precisely, whereas a percentage will depend on the browser's window size and screen resolution.

...contd

Repeat
Choose this option if you want the specified Marquee to repeat its scrolling, sliding or alternating effect.

Continuously
Select this option if you want the Marquee to repeat itself continuously while it is displayed in the browser's window.

Times
Set the number of times you would like the Marquee to repeat itself in the browser window.

Background Color
Choose a background colour to fill the Marquee region. This is useful for defining the exact size of the Marquee and how it aligns with the other text on the page.

HTML Commands

Although FrontPage's main feature is that it shields you from writing HTML code, there may be times when you want to insert some special HTML code straight into your page. To do this you need to see the page you are working on as an HTML document. You can do this from the Editor by choosing the HTML Command.

1 From the Editor, open the View menu and click on the HTML Command entry.

2 This dialogue box will open:

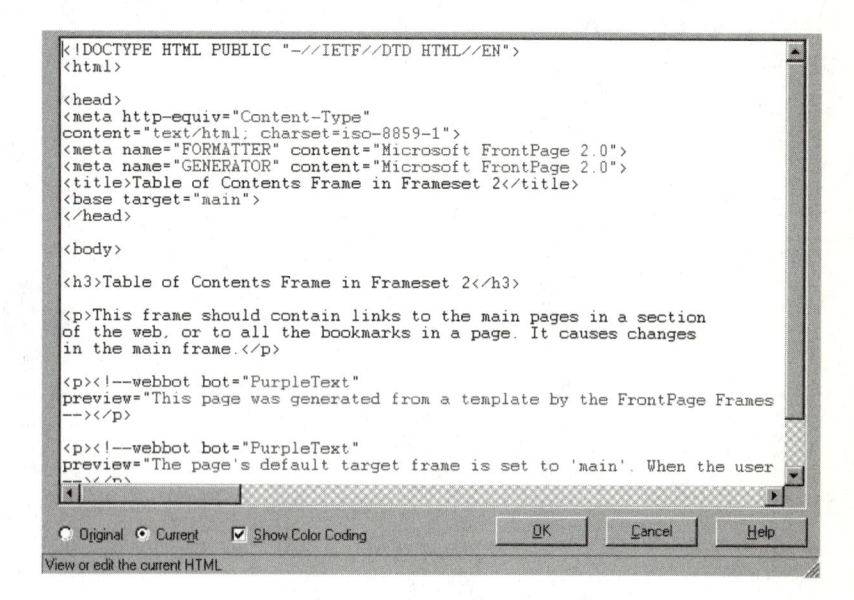

Original
Select this option if you want to view the page as it was before it was last saved.

Current
This displays the HTML code of the page as it appears at the moment in the Editor.

Show Color Coding
Select the colour coding for the HTML tags.

3. The Editor

...contd

BEWARE

As with all things that you copy from the Internet, be careful that the code that you are using isn't copyrighted. A quick e-mail to the site's creator will soon tell you if they will allow you to use their code on your pages.

As you surf the Internet you may come across a feature on a page that you just have to incorporate into the Web site that you are building. Your Web browser will be able to show the page as HTML code. You can then copy this to your Windows clipboard. When you have done this you can insert this into your FrontPage Web page where you like.

1 Open the page you want to add to in the FrontPage Editor. Then go to the Insert menu and click on 'HTML Markup'.

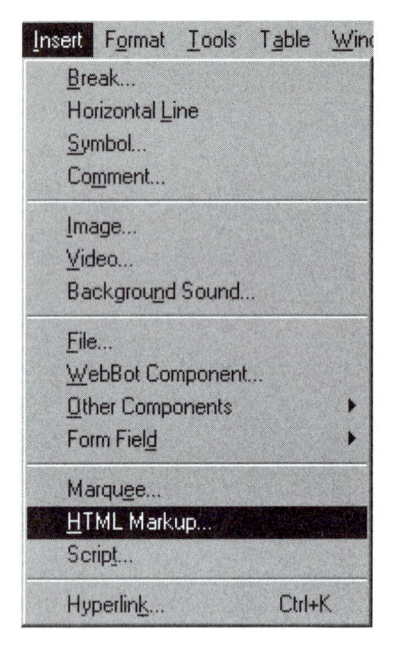

2 This dialogue will open. You can now paste the HTML code on the clipboard into the window.

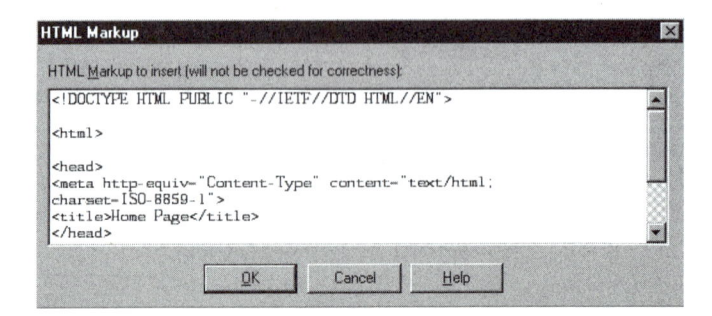

FrontPage in easy steps

...contd

BEWARE

FrontPage will not check the HTML code that you insert. It is up to you to make sure it is correct.

3 When you click OK, the HTML code will be added to your page. FrontPage will also insert an icon as you see here. This indicates that this code wasn't generated by FrontPage itself.

As you are adding HTML code from a source other than FrontPage, it is useful to leave yourself a note of what the code does and where you found it in the first place. You may need this information if you find that the code conflicts in any way with the code that FrontPage has generated. You can see how to leave a Comment for yourself that won't be visible in a Web browser on page 57.

The To Do List

After you have generated your Web site with a Wizard, you will be asked if you want to view the To Do List. Here you will find all the tasks that you need to carry out to complete your Web site before it is ready to be published. You can consult this dialogue box at any time. Click on 'Show To Do List' in the Tools menu of the Editor.

Activate this feature if you want to keep this window open as you complete each task.

Use this feature to show both completed and uncompleted tasks.

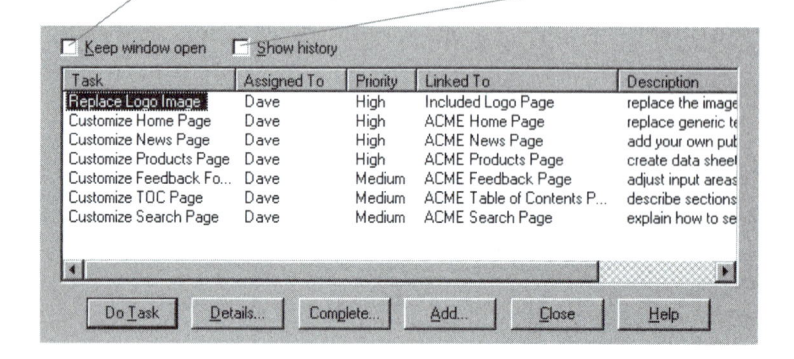

Task
This is the name of the task itself.

Assigned To
This shows who the task is assigned to. You may have one or more people working on your Web site. If you assign certain tasks to certain individuals, you can see at a glance who is doing what, and who has completed which tasks.

Priority
You can sort your tasks by priority – high priority at the top, moving to low priority at the bottom.

Completed
You will only see this column if you have ticked the Show History box at the top of the dialogue box.

...contd

Linked To
If you have more than one task assigned to a page you can sort them and display them in this column.

Description
A description can be added manually by you or by a Wizard when you build a Web site. You can edit the descriptions at any time.

You will also notice that there are a number of buttons running across the bottom of this dialogue box. Their functions are explained below.

Do Task
FrontPage will open the page on which this task needs to be completed. You can then enter text or graphics as needed. In this case it is the insertion of the company logo on one of the Web pages.

> Company Logo Comment -- replace with your logo image

HANDY TIP — **If you have assigned an editor to all of your file formats, you will want the appropriate editor to open automatically when you click on a graphic. You saw how to do this in Chapter Two, on pages 42-44.**

Details
If the description of the task in the window isn't detailed enough, you can ask FrontPage to give you more information.

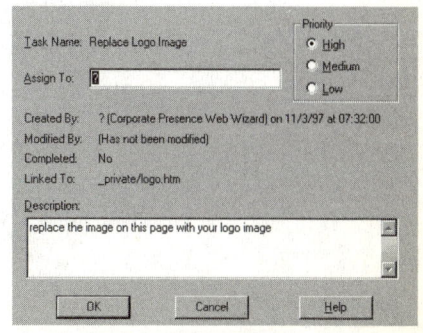

3. The Editor   **65**

...contd

Complete

When you have completed the task, you can tell FrontPage to keep track of what there is left to do. Also, you can see at a glance what you have completed and what remains to be done, if you have activated the Show History feature.

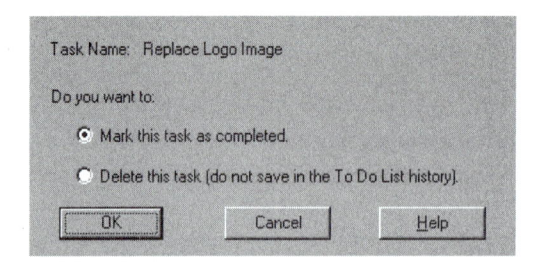

Add

As you design your Web pages, you can add tasks to the list as you go. The dialogue box is very similar to the Details box. You can assign the task a priority, as well as a description. You then know exactly what has to be done to which page.

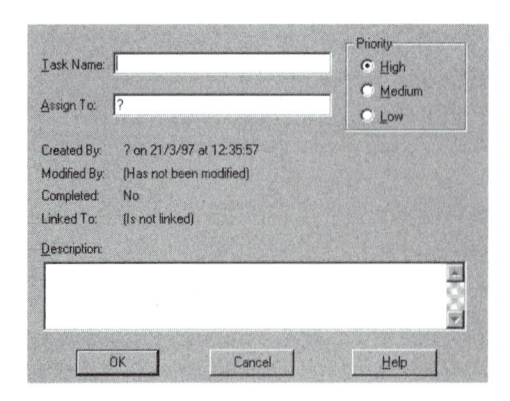

Frames

The use of frames can be seen on a large number of Web pages these days. They allow you to make your pages instantly more interesting, at the same time allowing your visitor to navigate your page with the least amount of fuss. FrontPage supports frames through its Frames Wizard. You can build a page with a variety of different frame layouts that you can then use in the Editor to place your information in.

1. From the Editor, open the File menu and click on the 'New' entry.

2. This dialogue box will open. Scroll down the list until you see the 'Frames Wizard' entry. Double-click on this now.

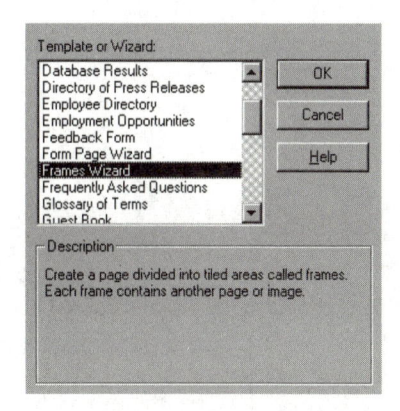

3. You will now enter the Frames Wizard. The first screen you see will ask you if you want to use one of the preprogrammed templates that is supplied with FrontPage. If, however, you want more control of your layout, you can choose the 'Make a custom grid' option. Here you can specify the exact layout of the frames on your page.

3. The Editor

...contd

For this example select the 'Pick a template' option. You can see how to set up a custom frame layout later in this chapter

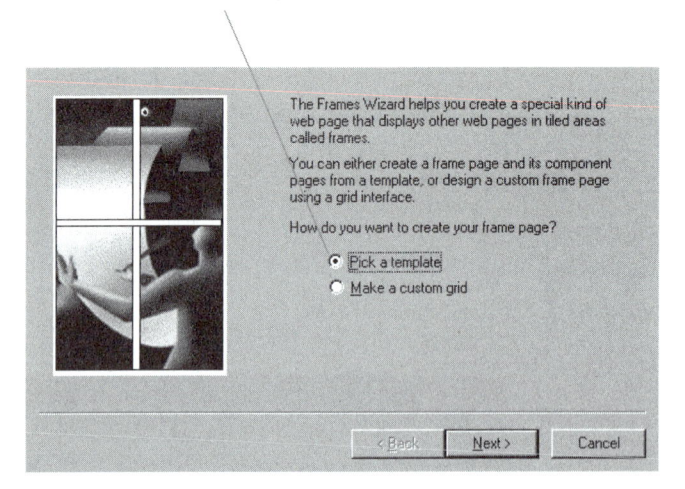

The Frames Wizard helps you create a special kind of web page that displays other web pages in tiled areas called frames.

You can either create a frame page and its component pages from a template, or design a custom frame page using a grid interface.

How do you want to create your frame page?

- ◉ Pick a template
- ○ Make a custom grid

4 If you now scroll through the options in the window in this frame, you will see the variety of frame layouts that FrontPage offers. If you click on an entry, the diagram of the frame layout in the left of the window will change. Choose a layout that suits the information that your page contains – in this case, a simple Table of Contents.

Select a frame set layout from the list of templates below.

Layout:
- Banner with nested Table of Contents
- Main document plus footnotes
- **Navigation bars with internal Table of Contents**
- Top-down three-level hierarchy
- Navigation bars with internal Table of Contents
- Nested three-level hierarchy
- Simple Table of Contents

Description:
Creates static navigation bars at the top and bottom, with an interior Table of Contents for the main frame.

68 FrontPage in easy steps

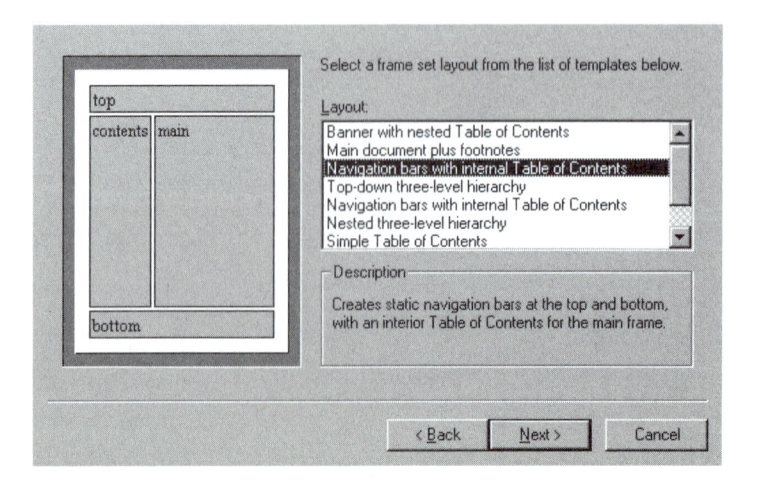

...contd

5 Some of your visitors may be using a browser that doesn't support frames. In this case, you can allocate an alternative frame-free page which can be accessed from the page with frames. This is much the same as you did with ordinary Web page graphics, where you can assign another page or graphic to the page your visitor is looking at. Type the URL in the box in this dialogue and FrontPage will insert this page instead of the frames.

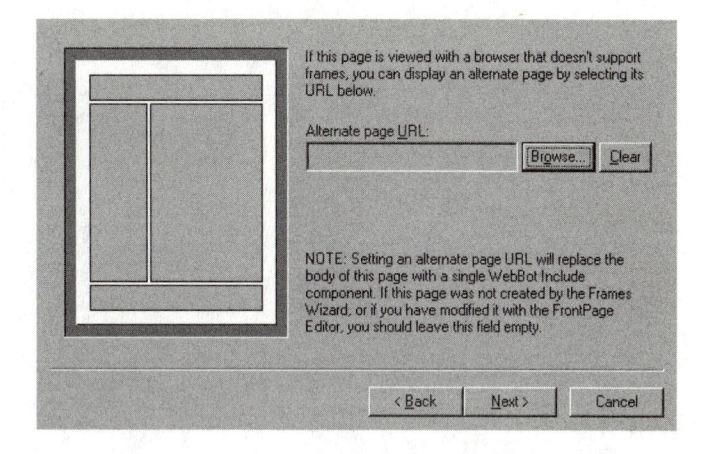

6 Type the frame name and URL, and then click 'Finish'. You have now created the frames on your Web page.

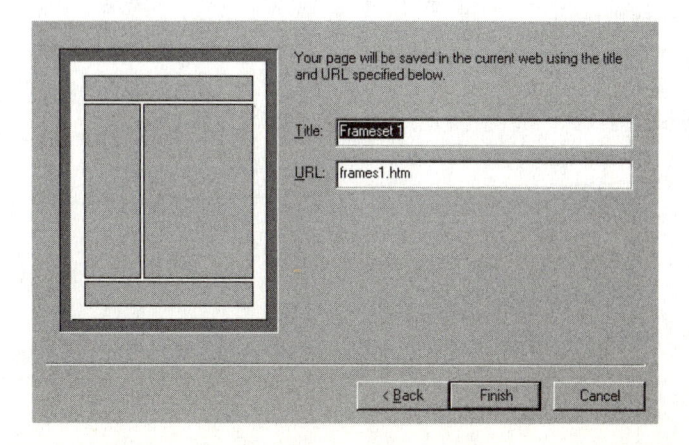

3. The Editor

69

Creating a Custom Frame

If you feel that the preset frame types are not suitable for your Web page, FrontPage gives you complete control over the creation of custom frames.

Open the Editor as you did before and choose the Frames Wizard (see page 67). You will see the screen from step 3 in the last section (page 68). If you choose 'Make a custom grid' you will see this dialogue box open. Enter the number of rows and columns you would like on your page, and click 'Next' to move to the next screen.

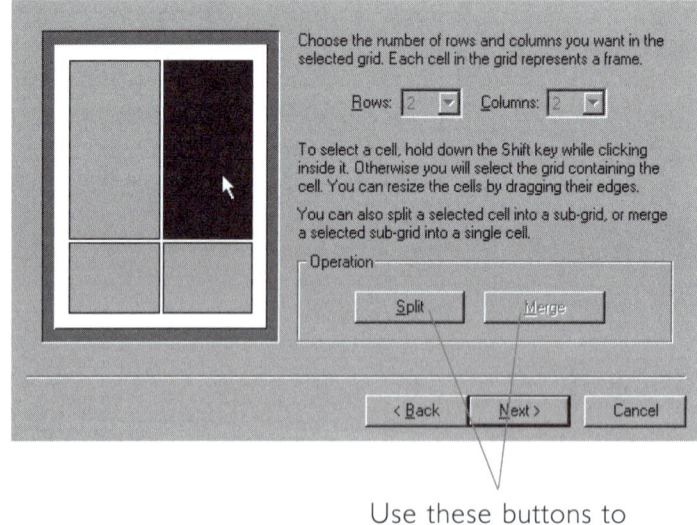

BEWARE

Try not to get too carried away with the number of frames you use. They are there to help visitors navigate your site, not confuse them!

Use these buttons to either split a cell or merge a cell back to its former size and shape.

70 FrontPage in easy steps

...contd

2 This is the Edit Frame Attributes dialogue box. Here you enter all of the settings that will be used in relation to each of the frames you have created on the page. Each one is independent. Clicking on it will activate it and allow you to enter its settings or attributes.

Enter the URL of the page that should be used for the contents of the selected frame. You can click Browse to choose a page from the currently open Web or enter the URL of another page.

Enter the name you will use when referring to the frame.

You can set the amount of space to leave around the frame. Enter this in pixels.

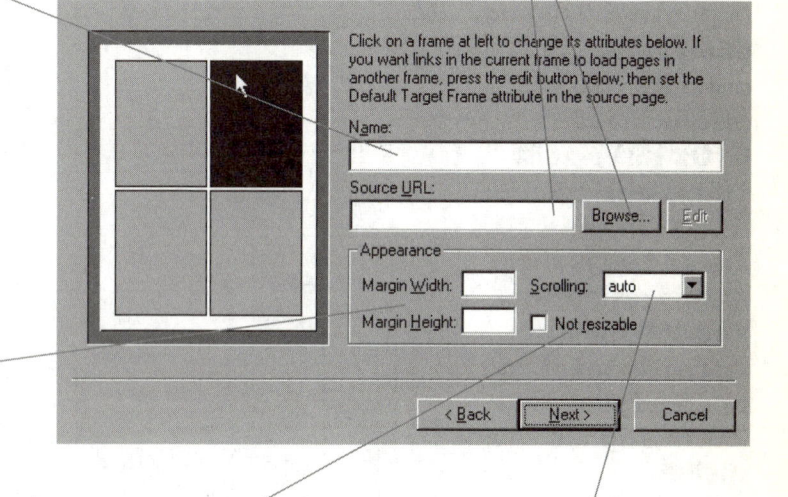

Think carefully before enabling this function. If you activate it your visitor will not be able to resize the frame windows in their browser.

If the page you specify for a frame contains a great deal of information, your visitor will need a scroll bar to see all of it.

3. The Editor

71

...contd

3 As with the last section, you will need to specify a page that can be used instead of this one if any of your visitors don't have a browser that can view frames. Enter its URL here, and then click 'Next'.

> **HANDY TIP**
>
> If you use any graphics as part of your frames, remember that users may view them at a low resolution. Try and design your graphics to a resolution of 640x480 pixels. This is also true for frames in general. Try and view them at this resolution. You will then instantly see if you can read the information in them easily.

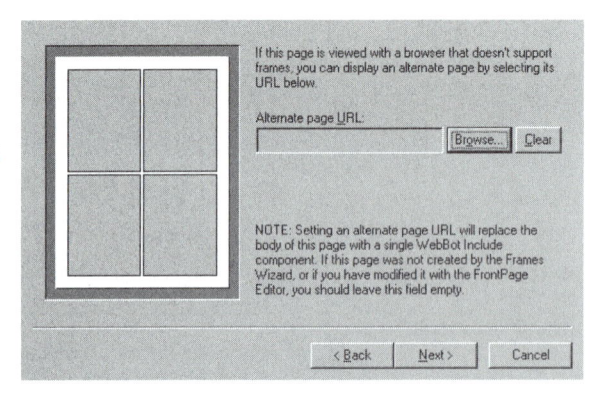

4 This is the last screen of this Wizard. Enter the title of the page (try and choose something that you can remember easily) and its URL.

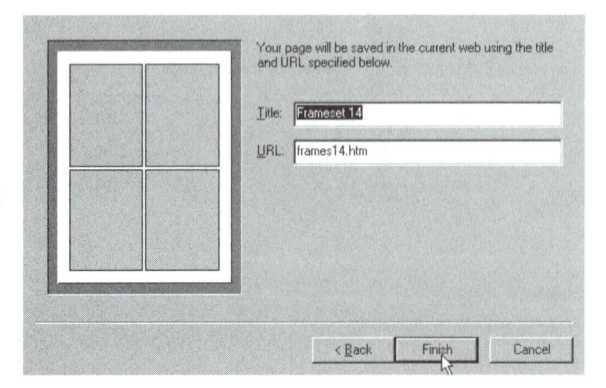

72 FrontPage in easy steps

Text Files

When you ask FrontPage to import a text file, you have the option of how the text will be formatted in the Editor. This will be done automatically when you have selected the type of formatting you want. The text will then be converted into a new HTML file ready for importing into your Web site.

1 From the Editor, choose File and Open, or click on this icon.

2 This dialogue will open. Click on the Other Location tab, and then on the Browse button. You will now see the usual file location dialogue box that you should be familiar with from other programs on your PC.

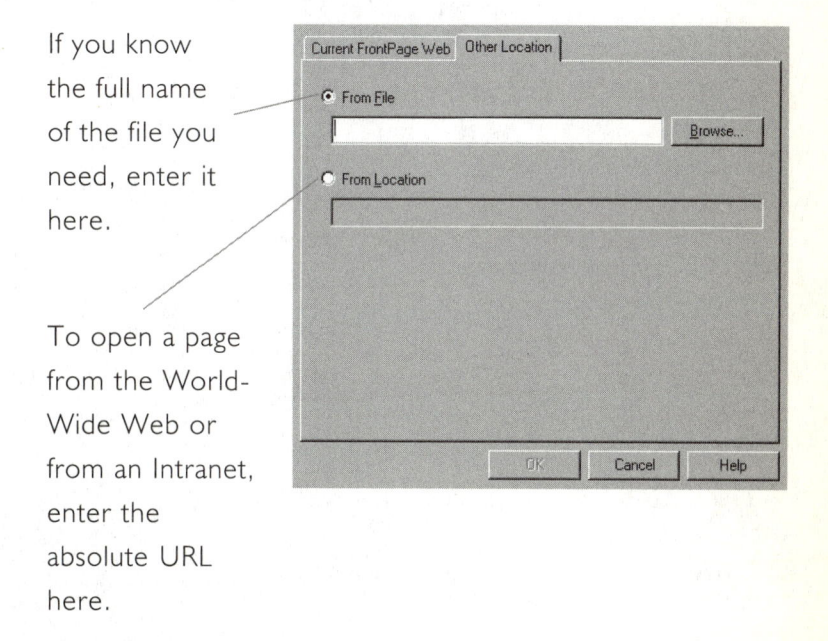

If you know the full name of the file you need, enter it here.

To open a page from the World-Wide Web or from an Intranet, enter the absolute URL here.

3. The Editor **73**

...contd

3. Choose the kind of file that you want to import from the drop-down list – in this case an ordinary text file. You can search for the file you want in the usual way in the window. When you have found it, double-click on it and the next dialogue will pop open.

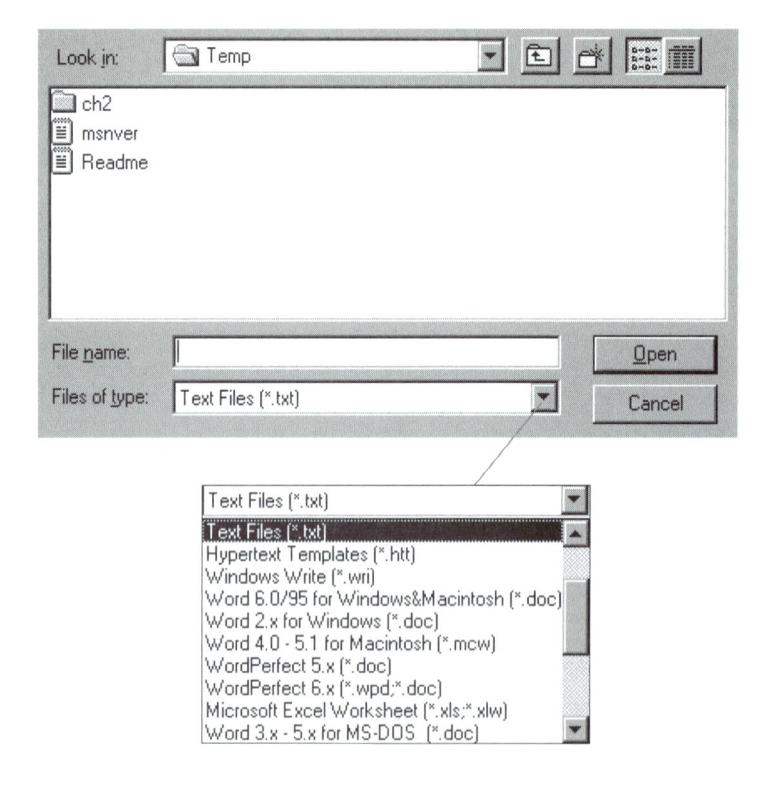

4. As you can see, FrontPage gives you complete control over how the text you are importing will be formatted on your Web page.

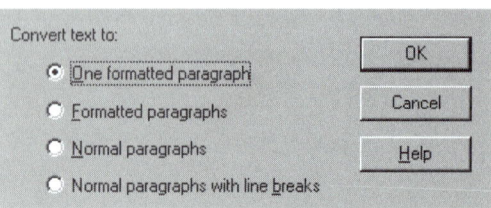

...contd

One formatted paragraph
This option converts the text to one single paragraph of monospaced text. All spaces and line breaks are shown.

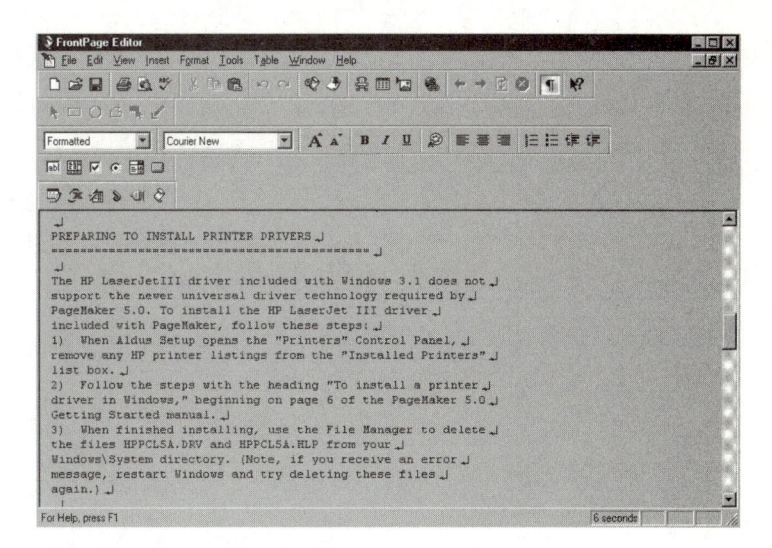

Formatted paragraphs
Converts each paragraph of text to multiple formatted paragraphs.

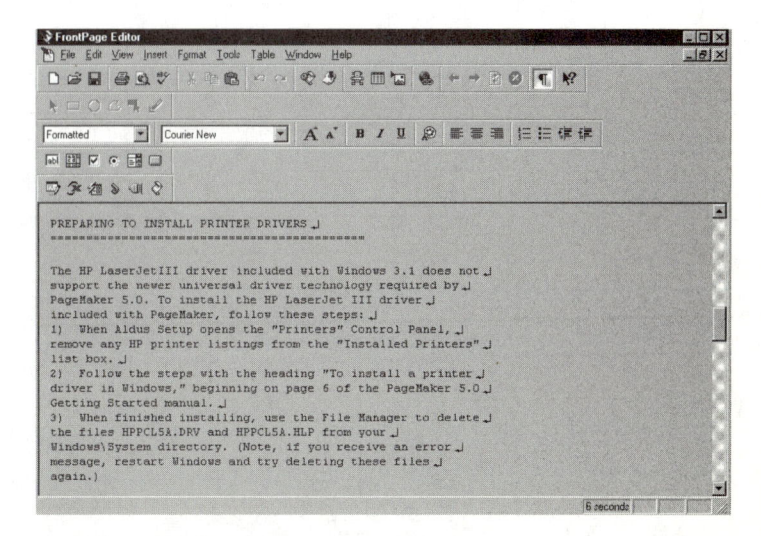

3. The Editor   75

...contd

Normal paragraphs
Converts each paragraph to normal text. No line breaks are shown.

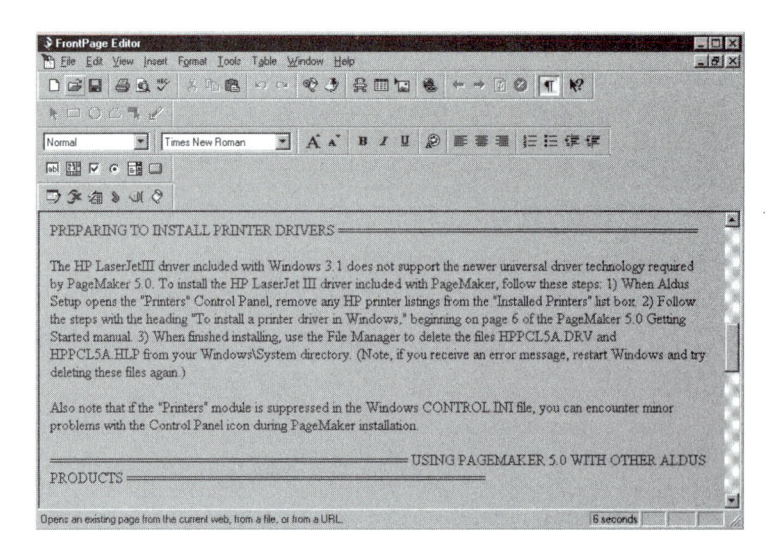

Normal paragraphs with line breaks
Converts each paragraph to normal text and preserves the line endings by inserting line breaks at the end of each line.

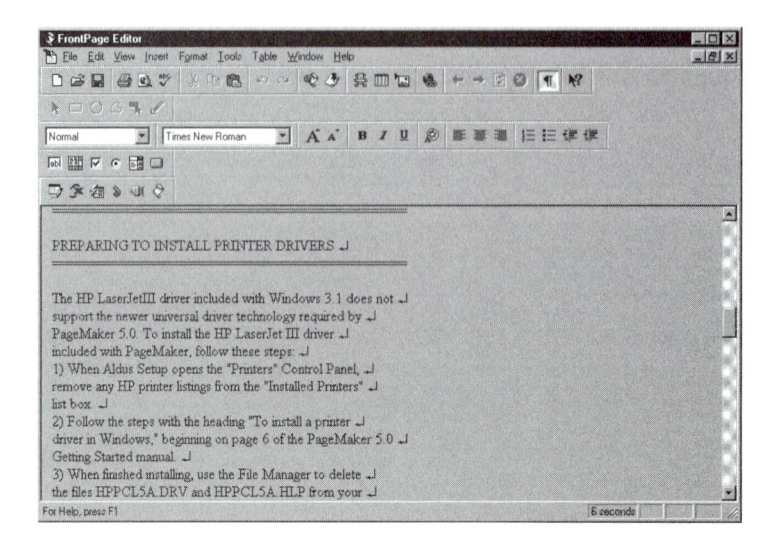

CHAPTER FOUR

Wizards and Templates

This chapter covers the powerful features of Templates and Wizards. With these tools you can create professional-looking Web sites with no programming knowledge whatsoever.

Covers

Page Templates 78
Wizards 81
Web Templates 87

Page Templates

Templates should not be confused with Wizards. Wizards are software modules that you can use to create a complex series of pages that can be added to your Web site. You will have seen one of these in action in Chapter One, in the generation of the Corporate Presence Web site in the Explorer. You won't be asked a series of questions, as in most cases the template is not customisable up-front. It simply provides a framework for you to work with.

There are 30 page templates currently supplied with FrontPage. Use these to create the extra pages that you need to make your site useful as well as interesting. You can create all the pages you need in one session, or build your site as you go. At all times FrontPage allows you to manipulate the information that is contained in each of the pages with the least amount of effort.

1 Open the Editor and choose 'New' from the File menu.

2 Choose one of the templates in the window – in this case the Guest Book template.

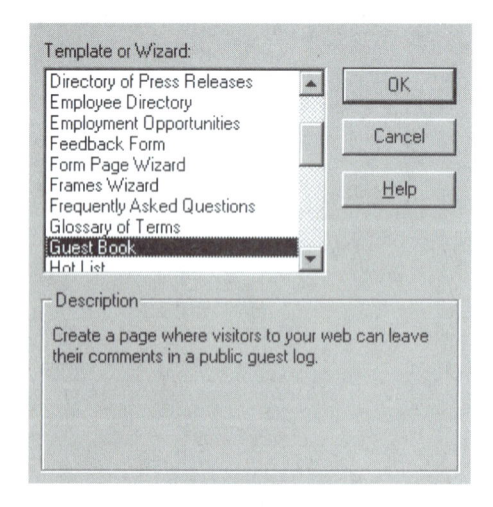

3 When you click on the template you want to use, it will be created straight away. Remember, these are not like Wizards where you answer questions as each dialogue box pops up. The template will open in the Editor for you to enter your own information.

...contd

Custom Templates

FrontPage does not limit you to the Wizards and Templates that it provides. You can create your own template and save it for future use.

1. Choose New from the File menu in the Editor.

2. Select 'Normal Page' from the list of templates and click OK.

3. When the page has loaded you can insert all the information you need. When you have done so, go back to the File menu and choose 'Save As'.

4. This dialogue box will appear. Click on 'As Template'.

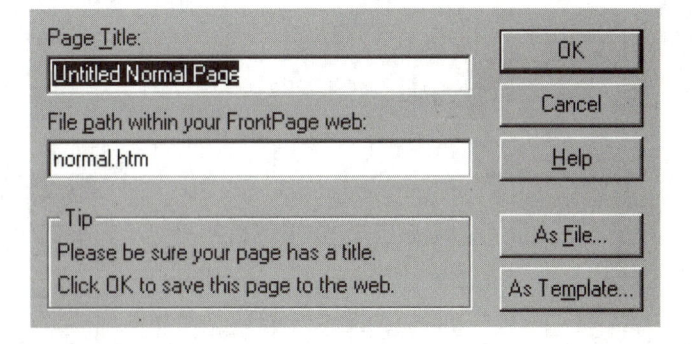

5. Enter a name for your new template and any comments, then click OK. This template will now be added to your list, which you will see each time you select 'New' in the Editor.

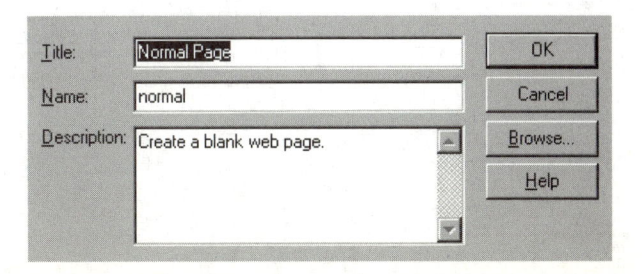

4. Wizards and Templates

...contd

6 Choose a set of pages that you want to keep as a template. In this case it is a Home page created with another template. You can change some of the settings to your liking and then re-save it as a new template.

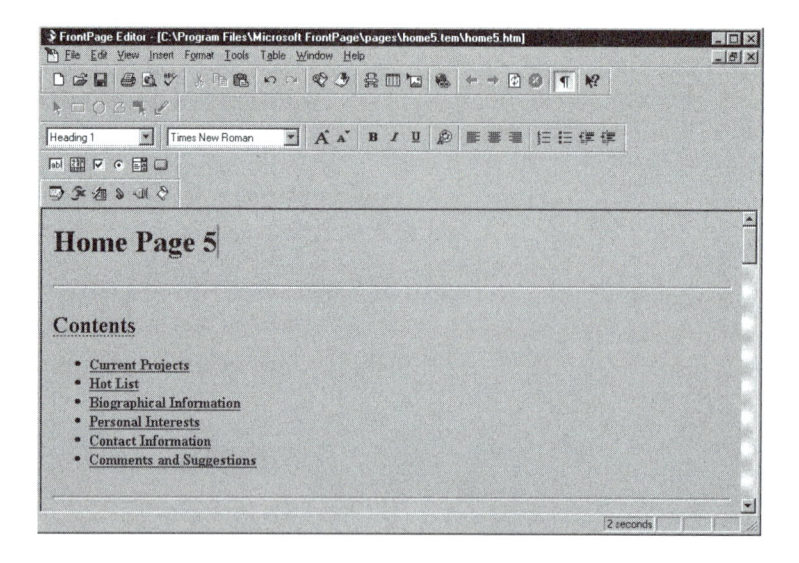

7 If you now click on 'New' from the File menu the usual template dialogue box will open. If you scroll down the list you will see your new Home page as an entry. You can now use this as a template for future web pages of this design.

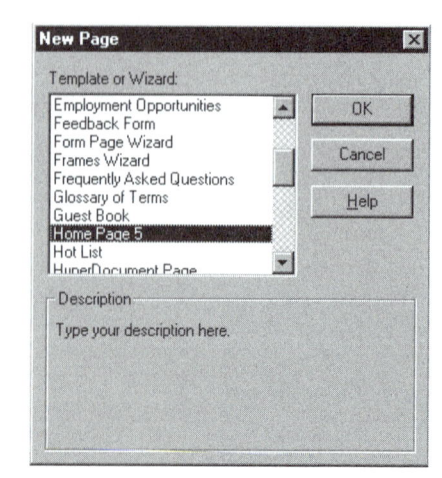

Wizards

Most users of Windows will by now be familiar with the concept of the Wizard. By simply answering a series of questions, you can install software or with FrontPage create a complete Web site as we did in Chapter One. These 'helper' applications speed up the creation of Web pages and other elements that go to make up your Web site.

Page Wizards

1. Most of the main Wizards are accessed from the Explorer. This is how we created the Corporate Presence Web site in Chapter One. Use these to create the bulk of the Web pages that you need for your site.

2. If you now go to the Editor and click on 'New' in the File menu as you did previously, you will see the familiar Wizard and Template dialogue box. As well as the templates, there are a number of Wizards you can use.

3. For an example, click on 'Personal Home Page Wizard'.

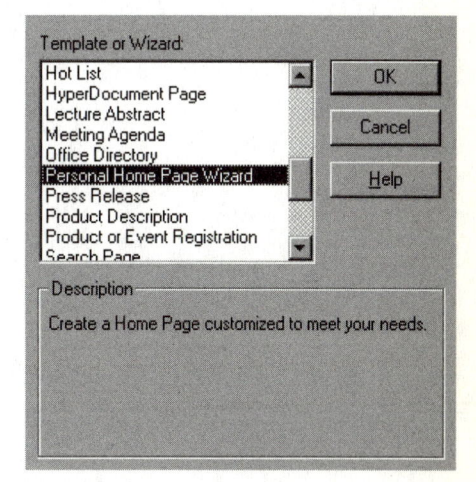

4. Wizards and Templates

...contd

4 Choose the sections that your Home page will have.

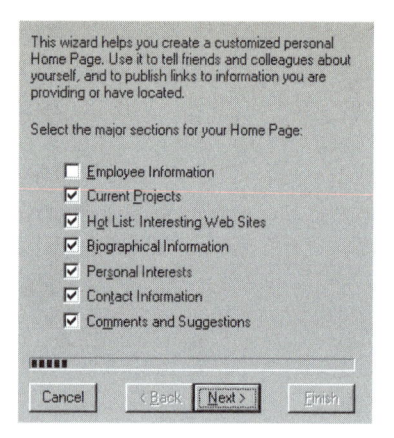

5 Type in the title of your Home page.

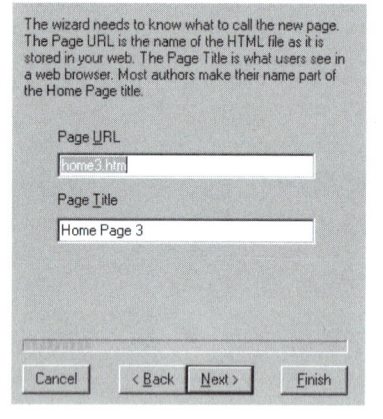

6 Enter as many projects as you want in the window.

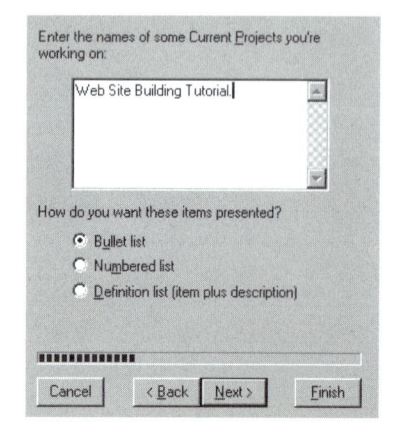

...contd

7 Set how your current Hot list will be displayed on your page.

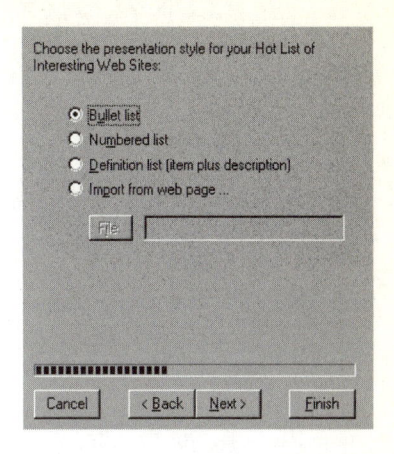

8 Choose the format that best suits your Web site.

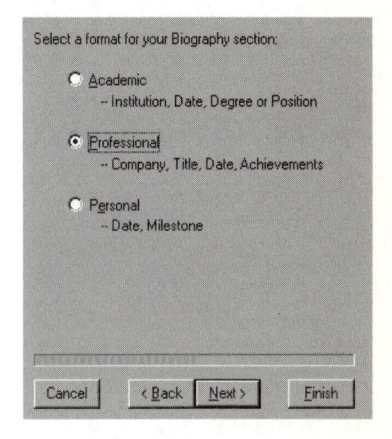

9 Enter as many interests as you like, and choose how they will be displayed on the page.

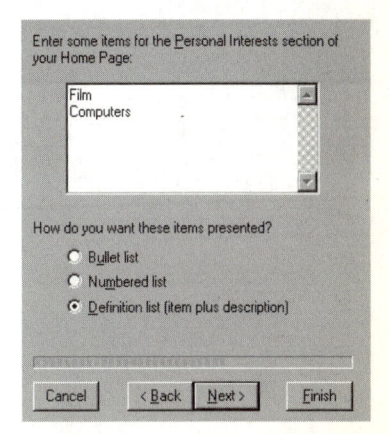

4. Wizards and Templates 83

...contd

10 Enter all this information for inclusion on your Home page.

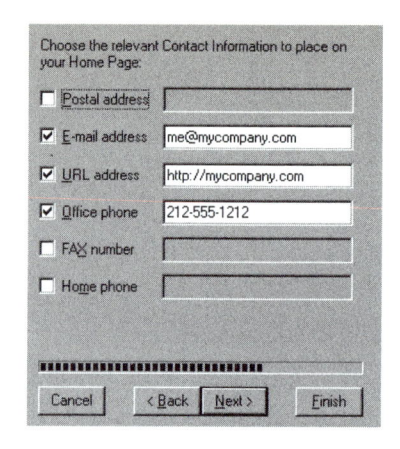

11 Choose how you want to store information that you gather from your Web site.

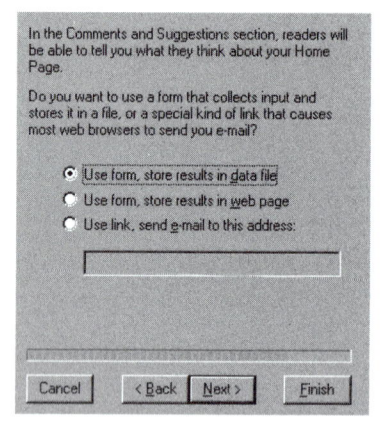

12 You can set the order in which pages are created on your site. Click on an item then click on the Up or Down buttons to change the position of that item in the list.

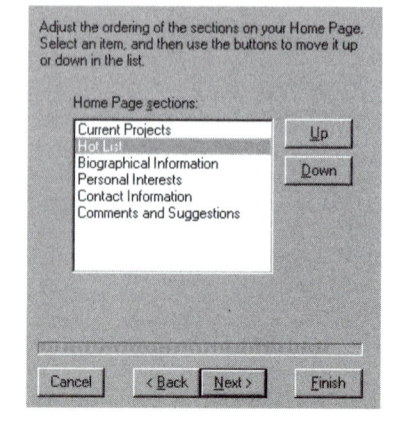

...contd

13 You have now given
FrontPage all the
information it needs to
create your home page. If
you want to change any of
the information that you
have entered, click on
'Back' to return to the
appropriate screen. If not,
click 'Finish' to build your
Web pages.

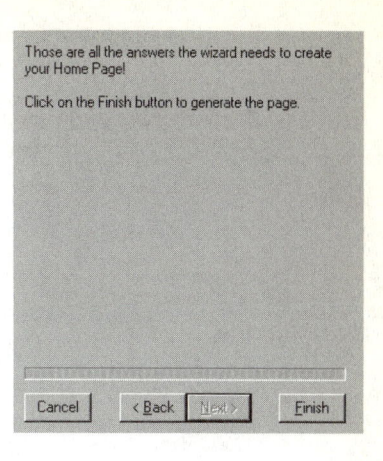

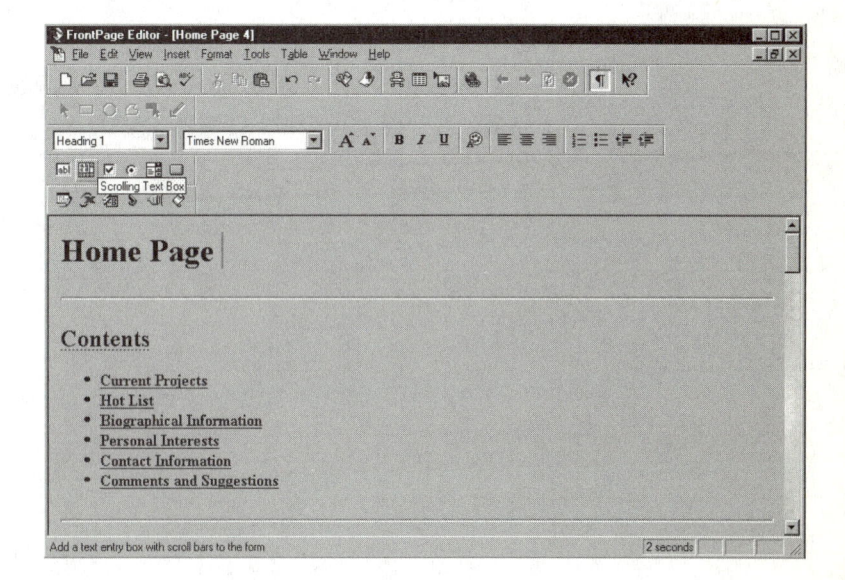

After you have clicked 'Finish', FrontPage will build the
Web site. When it is finished you will see the first page
open in the Editor. You now have full control over the text
and graphics as you would with any page created with
FrontPage.

4. Wizards and Templates

...contd

As you can see, the use of Wizards is very easy. All the FrontPage Wizards operate in this way. Most of the information that you will be asked for in any dialogue box you should be able to enter straight away. If you don't have this to hand at the time, you can abort the Wizard and start it again when you do have the information it requested.

Wizards can also be combined in a single Web site to create some very complex sites. In this case it is advisable to build your pages one at a time. You can then see how the site looks and navigates before you create the next set of pages. If at any time you don't like the layout, or you have forgotten to put something in a Wizard, you can create another one and simply replace the existing pages with the new ones.

At no time are you constrained with the design or layout of the pages, or the structure of the whole Web site. Of course, you can only create pages with the Wizards provided, but they offer a wide range of options, some of which should suit your needs. If not, you can always customise a series of pages and save them as a template.

Web Templates

Web templates should not be confused with Web Wizards. The templates that you can use to create a Web site are self-contained. They do not ask you a series of questions, apart from the name of the Web you want to create. They are a fast means of creating a series of Web pages. As always, you have full control over the pages once they have been created, as you can open them in the Editor.

1 From the Explorer, select 'New' from the File drop-down menu, or click on this icon.

```
New                    ▶  Folder
Open FrontPage Web...     FrontPage Web...  Ctrl+N
Close FrontPage Web
```

2 This dialogue box appears.

BEWARE

If the file that you want to import into your existing Web site is already there, it will be overwritten. You will see a warning box pop up to give you a chance to cancel this operation if you don't want to replace the existing file.

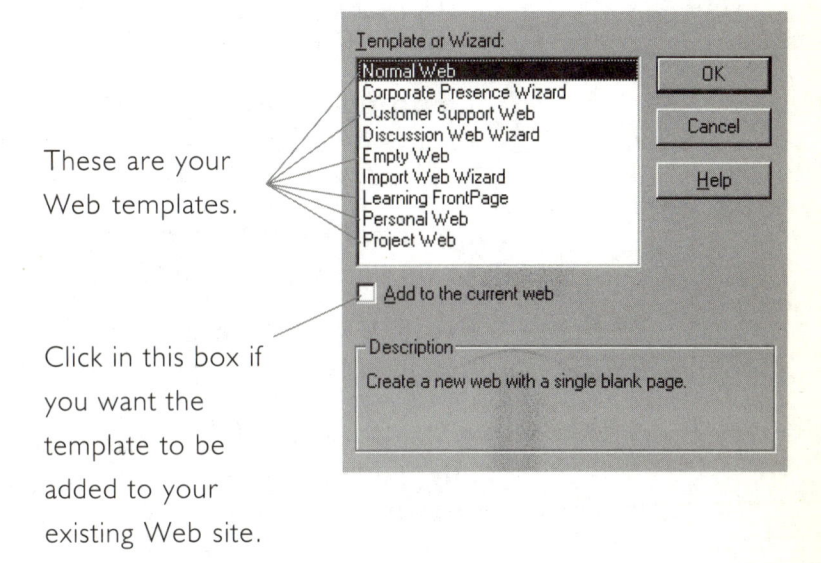

These are your Web templates.

Click in this box if you want the template to be added to your existing Web site.

Template or Wizard:
- Normal Web
- Corporate Presence Wizard
- Customer Support Web
- Discussion Web Wizard
- Empty Web
- Import Web Wizard
- Learning FrontPage
- Personal Web
- Project Web

☐ Add to the current web

Description: Create a new web with a single blank page.

4. Wizards and Templates

87

...contd

Normal Web (template)
Creates a Web with a single blank page.

Corporate Presence Web (Wizard)
Creates a professional Internet presence.

Customer Service Support Web (template)
Creates pages that can help you provide a better level of support for your customers. This is especially useful for software companies.

Discussion Web (Wizard)
Creates a discussion Web with text search, tables of contents and threads.

Empty Web (template)
Creates a new FrontPage Web with nothing in it.

Import Web (Wizard)
Creates a Web that contains documents from a local or remote file system.

Learning FrontPage Tutorial (template)
Creates a Web that uses the templates that can be used with the 'Getting Started With FrontPage' manual.

Personal Web (template)
Creates a simple personal home page.

Project Web (template)
Creates a Web for a particular project.

When the Web template has finished it will open the site into the Explorer. You can now open a page in the FrontPage Editor, enter your text and place your graphics.

CHAPTER FIVE

Designing Your Pages

Once you have created the Web site of your choice and have used templates and wizards to add the pages that you think you will need, now is the time to think about the design of the pages themselves. This chapter looks at how you can place elements such as text and graphics on your pages.

Covers

Text	90
Page Properties	92
Opening Pages	93
Images	95
Image Properties	97
Video	98
Hotspots	99
Transparent Colours	101
Sound	102

Text

Text is one of the simplest elements to add to a Web page. In the FrontPage Editor it is simply a matter of clicking on the page in the area you want the text to appear, and starting to type. You will be familiar with this from using your word-processor.

1. In the Editor, open a page to which you want to add some text.

2. These are the icons which give you a shortcut to changing the font style – to italic for instance – and also some simple formatting commands.

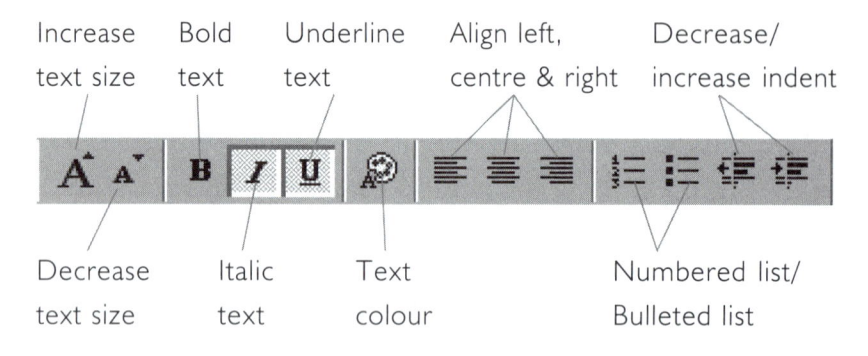

Increase text size | Bold text | Underline text | Align left, centre & right | Decrease/increase indent

Decrease text size | Italic text | Text colour | Numbered list/Bulleted list

3. Under the Format menu in the Editor select 'Font'. This dialogue box opens.

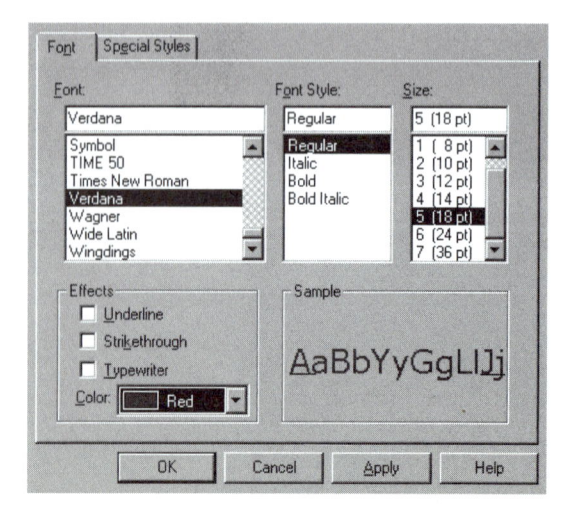

FrontPage in easy steps

...contd

This dialogue box gives you complete control over the fonts that you use on your pages. Choose a font, its size and any style you like. Here is a blank page with some text entered in various sizes and styles.

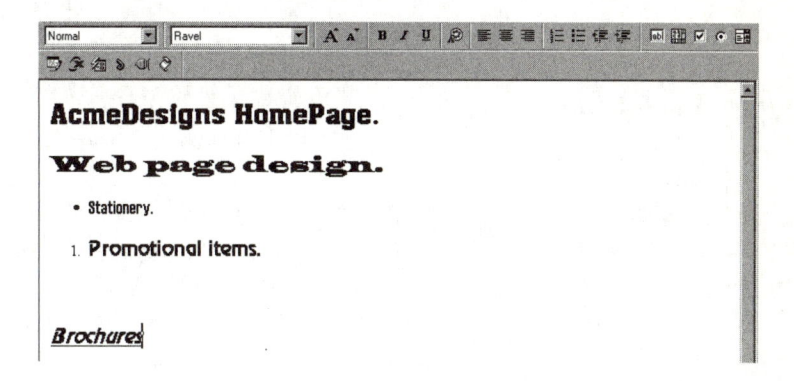

4 The commands that you can click on are also duplicated in the drop-down menus. For instance, to change the paragraph format of some text, click on the Format menu and choose 'Bullets and Numbering'.

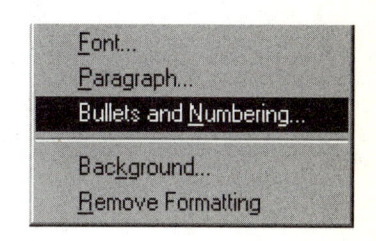

5 The dialogue box below opens. You can now choose the type of numbering you want to use. This kind of ease of use is available throughout FrontPage.

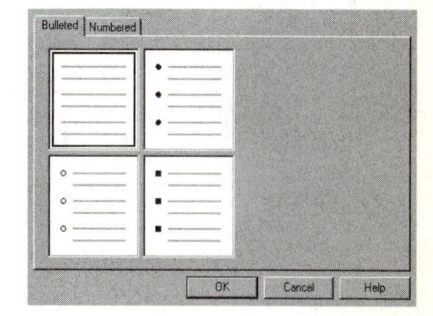

5. Designing Your Pages

91

Page Properties

Even if you have already chosen some of the layout properties of your page when you created them with a Wizard, you still have full control over each page's layout.

From within the Editor, choose 'Page Properties' from the File menu. An alternative is to right-click on the page: clicking on 'Properties' in the pop-up menu will open the same dialogue box. You will see this screen.

REMEMBER — **Each time you open this dialogue box you must have a page loaded into the Editor.**

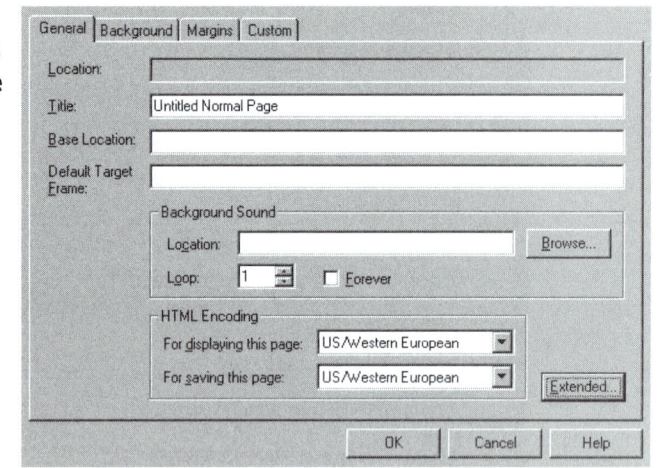

This screen gives you complete control over the look of your pages. You can change the background colour and the colour that text appears in when it is a hyperlink, for instance. You can also specify sound and any background image you would like displayed. Clicking the 'Help' button explains in detail what each of the properties you can set will do to your page.

92 FrontPage in easy steps

Opening Pages

You can open files from your system that were not created using FrontPage itself. You can use the Windows file system in the usual way to locate and load the file you need. However, FrontPage treats various file formats in different ways.

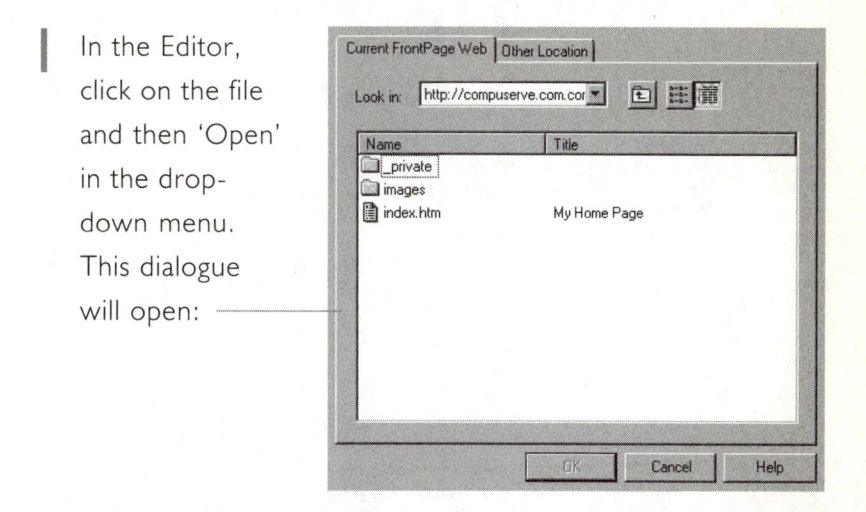

1 In the Editor, click on the file and then 'Open' in the drop-down menu. This dialogue will open:

2 Click on 'Other Location'. This dialogue will open. Click on 'Browse'.

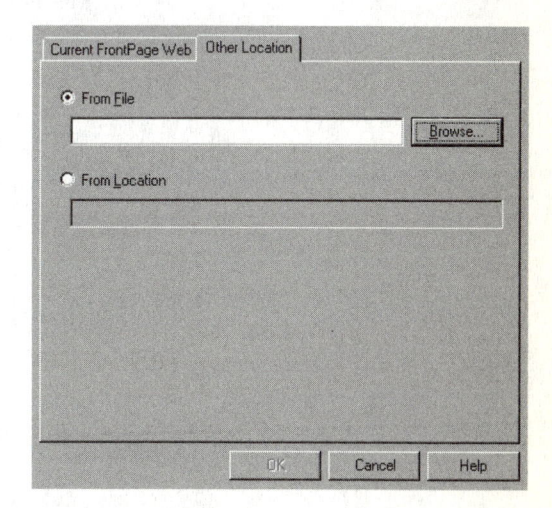

This now opens the familiar Windows file selector that you can see on the following page. You can now look for the file that you want to import into your Web page.

5. Designing Your Pages **93**

...contd

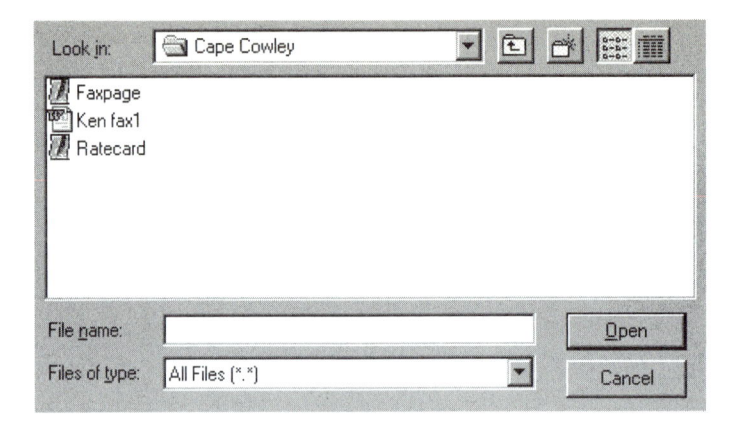

For this example, choose a text file – perhaps one that you have created in your word-processor.

3 When you click on the text file to import it, FrontPage detects this and opens this dialogue.

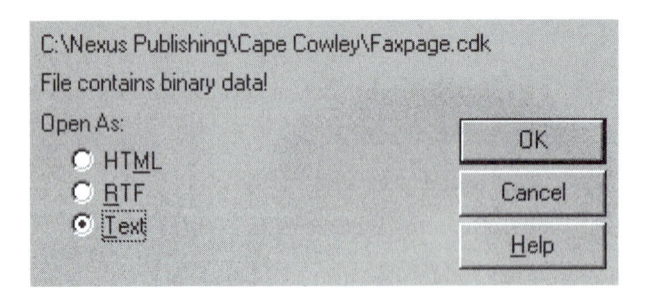

4 This dialogue will pop up to allow you to select how the text will be formatted when it is imported into the page.

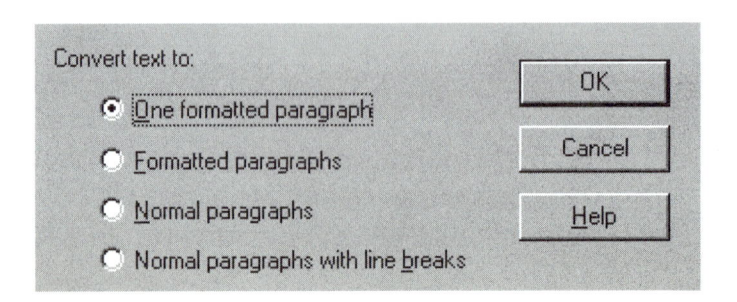

Images

Always be aware of the copyright of the images that you use on your Web site. You cannot freely scan or save images from other Web sites without the permission of their original creators.

Graphics make any Web page stand out. Logos and illustrations, when well-chosen and placed on a page, make it come alive. This is certainly the case if you are putting together a business Web site. But this is equally true of a personal Web page. FrontPage allows the manipulation of graphics so you can import them straight onto your page.

The Internet generally uses two types of graphic formats: JPEG (Joint Photographic Expert Group) and GIF (Graphics Interchange Format). JPEGs use data compression, as they are mostly used for high-quality photographic images, and support 256 or more colours. GIFs, on the other hand, are best suited to images that contain less than 256 colours. They also use a different compression system.

1 To import a graphic, place the cursor where you want the graphic to appear. Open the Editor and choose 'Image' from the Insert menu.

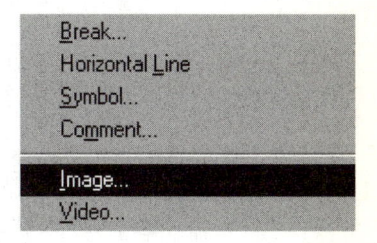

2 You will see this dialogue open. It allows you to load a graphic from a variety of locations. Click on 'Other Location' if you want to browse your hard drive or import the image from floppy disk. You also have the choice of using some of the ready-made clip art that you can import into your page.

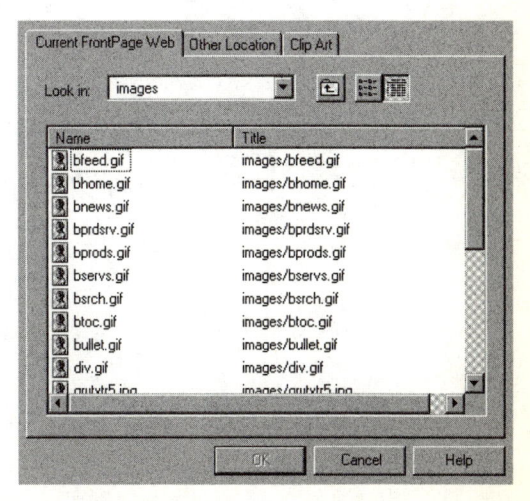

5. Designing Your Pages

...contd

3 For this example, choose the Clip Art tab. You will see the dialogue box below:

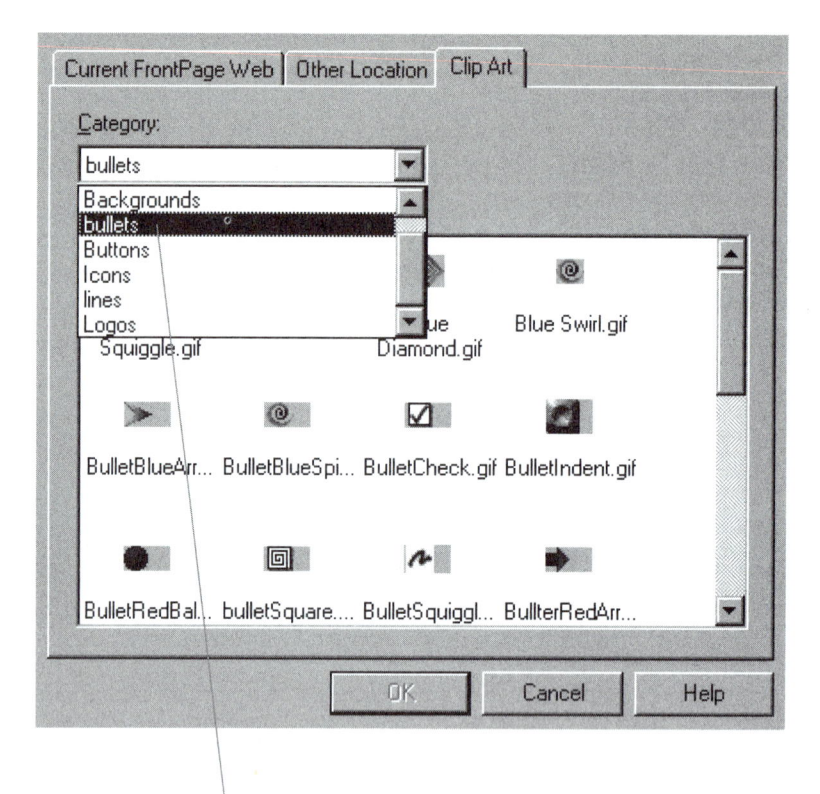

4 You have a choice of image categories. Choose one from the drop-down menu and then double-click on the image of your choice. It will now be imported into the Web page at the cursor point.

Image Properties

Once you have your graphic on your page, there are a variety of things that you can do with it.

1 If you right-click on the image, this pop-up menu will appear. Click on 'Image Properties'.

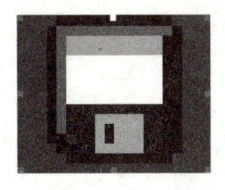

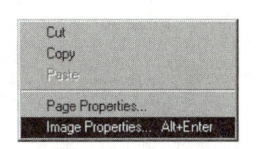

2 This is the Image Properties dialogue box:

Specify a small image to load into the user's browser while the main image is fetched from the server.

Set the image quality factor. 75 is the default.

HANDY TIP — **The quality of the image increases as compression decreases, but makes the image larger. The higher the number you enter in the Quality box, the lower the compression ratio.**

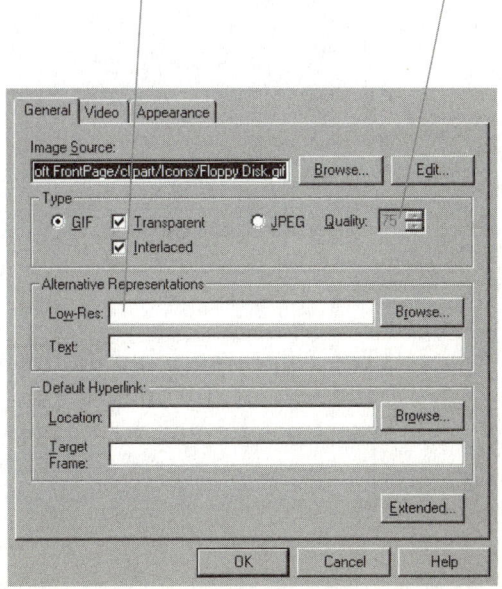

5. Designing Your Pages

97

Video

One of the advanced features that FrontPage allows you to have on your Web pages are animations. You can insert video footage into your page. The attributes of these images are set using this dialogue box.

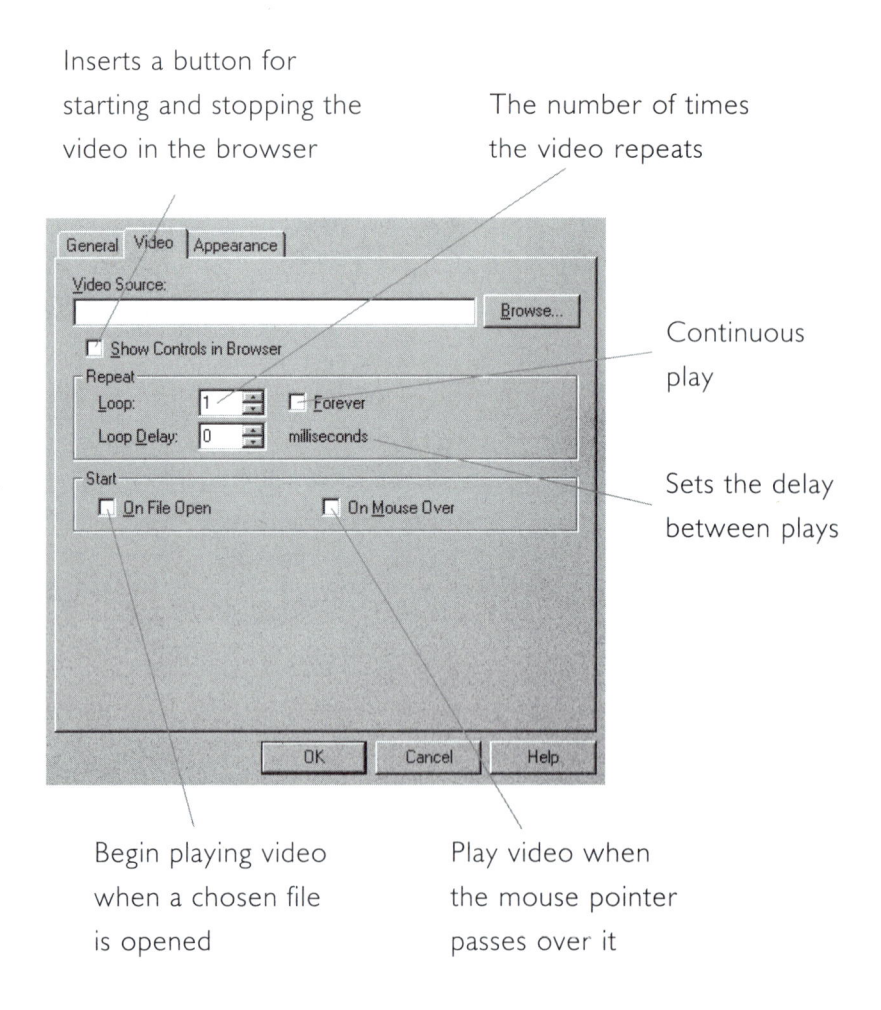

Inserts a button for starting and stopping the video in the browser

The number of times the video repeats

Continuous play

Sets the delay between plays

Begin playing video when a chosen file is opened

Play video when the mouse pointer passes over it

The Appearance tab on this dialogue box sets the layout and size of the images that you import. You can specify the exact position of the images as they appear on each page.

Hotspots

As the Web is interactive, your images can be too. On many Web sites that you have visited, you will have seen a graphic that has clickable elements: these are the hotspots that take you to another part of the site, as they have hyperlinks embedded within them.

These are the icons that you use to create your hotspot and also make an image transparent. If you cannot see them in the Editor, click on 'Image toolbar' from the View drop-down menu.

1. Make sure the image that you want to make into a hotspot is selected. You will see the Image toolbar become active when you do so.

2. Look at your image and decide the shape of the hotspot you want to create. If you have a notice-board graphic, for instance, you might want to make some of the notes on the board hotspots to take the visitor to that part of your site.

3. Choose one of the shapes you want to make your hotspot. The cursor will change to a pencil when you move it over your image.

...contd

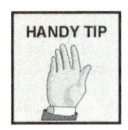

HANDY TIP — **If you move the hotspot but change your mind, hit the Esc key on your keyboard before you release the mouse button. This will return the hotspot to its original position.**

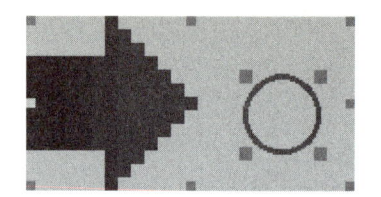

Here is an image that has had a circular hotspot drawn over it. You can move the hotspot around as you would any graphic file by activating it and then dragging it to its new location.

4 When you have drawn your hotspot this dialogue will open.

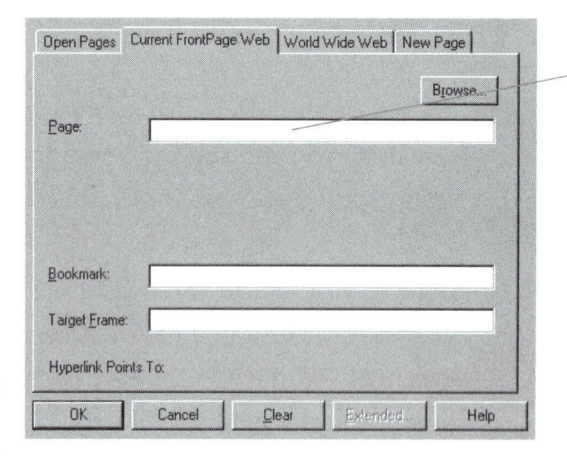

5 Enter the address of the Web page to which you want this hyperlink to lead.

HANDY TIP — **If the page that you are linking to doesn't exist yet, FrontPage will add this task to the To Do List to remind you.**

You can link the hotspot to a variety of pages, not just those contained on your web site. Links can be established with sites on the World Wide Web and even FTP (File Transfer Protocol), if there is some software for the visitor to download. Perhaps the hotspot was on a page of a product catalogue; you can link the image of the item to the Web site where the visitor can get hold of it.

100 FrontPage in easy steps

Transparent Colours

REMEMBER **You cannot make JPEG images transparent.**

The GIF image that you imported on the previous page could also be made transparent. This is simply making one of the colours of the image transparent so that the background colour shows through.

This is the icon in the image toolbar that you use to make a colour transparent.

BEWARE **If you load a JPEG image and attempt to make a colour transparent you will see a dialogue box warning you that the image will first be converted to GIF format. Make sure you wish the image to be converted before proceeding.**

1 Select the image that contains the colour you want to make transparent.

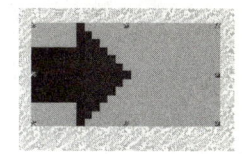

2 Click on the Make Transparent button.

3 Move the pointer over the image. You will notice that the mouse pointer changes shape to the Make Transparent pointer.

4 Click on the colour that you want to make transparent. If you have a background colour or pattern selected, this will now show through the image.

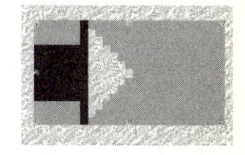

REMEMBER **Only one colour at a time can be transparent.**

You can now see that the selected colour in the image has been made transparent. The background colour shows through in all areas where that colour exists.

5. Designing Your Pages   **101**

Sound

You can add sound to your Web pages just as easily as you did with graphics. You must have the sound available either on your current Web page or elsewhere on your system, or you must know the URL of the sound you want to use.

1 Select 'Background Sound' from the Insert menu.

2 This dialogue will open.

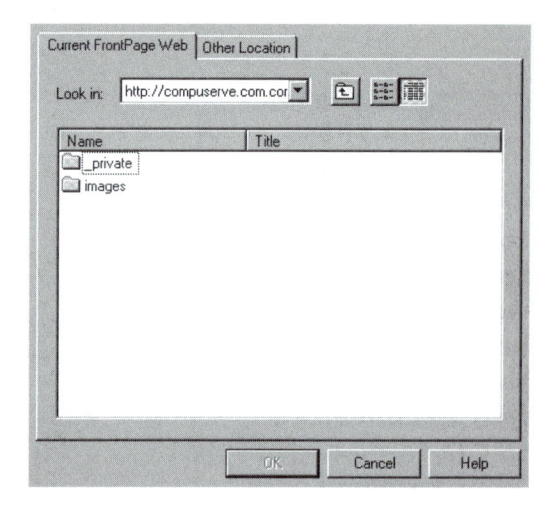

If you click on the 'Other Location' tab, you will be able to choose a file from your system using the usual Windows File Location dialogue box. If you don't have the sound you want to use, but know its absolute URL, then you can enter it here.

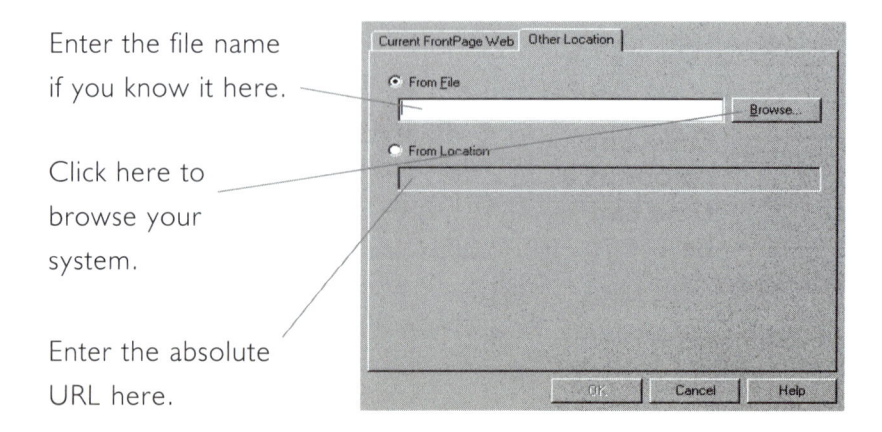

Enter the file name if you know it here.

Click here to browse your system.

Enter the absolute URL here.

CHAPTER SIX

WebBots

WebBots (or just 'Bots') are small programs that you can drop into your Web site to give it functions that would usually take a great deal of time to program manually. FrontPage is supplied with a wide range of Bots for you to use. This chapter introduces the WebBot and shows you how you can use them in your Web site.

Covers

Introduction	104
Search WebBot	105
Scheduled Image/Include WebBot	108
Substitution WebBot	110
Table of Contents WebBot	114
Timestamp WebBot	117
Registration WebBot	119

Introduction

The WebBot is an innovation that allows you to use advanced features as part of your Web pages. Without them, you would need to have an intimate knowledge of HTML coding, and one of the scripting languages such as Perl or JavaScript. WebBots do all the hard work for you. All you need to do is to set the parameters of the WebBot and decide in most cases how to place it on your page. The rest is taken care of.

WebBots are split into two types.

Client Bots

The client is the computer that is connected to the Internet and is looking at your pages. They are the computers of the visitors to your site. These WebBots add advanced functions to your pages such as inserting an image or other contents at specific times, or generating tables of contents. They are used as part of the overall design of your Web site. These Bots don't need the Server Extensions as they require no interaction with the visitor.

Server Bots

These WebBots are used when you want some interaction to take place between your site and the visitor. They are those Bots that request input from your visitors such as filling in a form or signing a visitors' book. If you didn't have these Bots you would have to go out and learn how to write custom scripts in JavaScript or VBScript! These Bots do need the Server Extensions to be installed on the server.

You can check that these are working with the Personal Web Server that is supplied with FrontPage. If all is well, you can publish your Web site to a remote server. As long as it has the FrontPage Server Extensions installed, your Web site should perform as it did on your computer. When your visitors input information or click on the Submit button, the information will be gathered by the server ready for you to access.

Search WebßBot

Any large Web site can be difficult to navigate if you haven't visited it before. You know the information you want is there, but don't know exactly where to look for it. A search engine is the answer. You may be familiar with these when searching the World Wide Web as a whole; they can, however, be used to great effect within your own Web site.

1 Open the page on which you want to insert the WebBot.

2 Set the cursor to the point on the page where you would like the top left-hand edge of the form to appear.

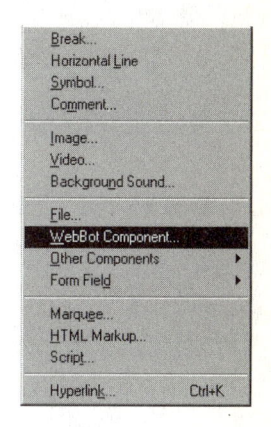

3 From the Editor choose the Insert menu and then click on 'WebBot' Component. This dialogue appears. Double-click on the Search entry.

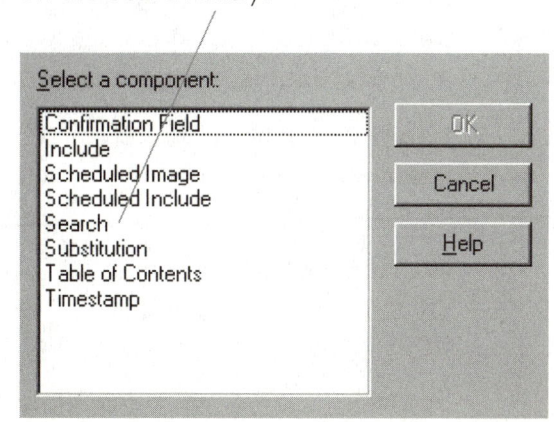

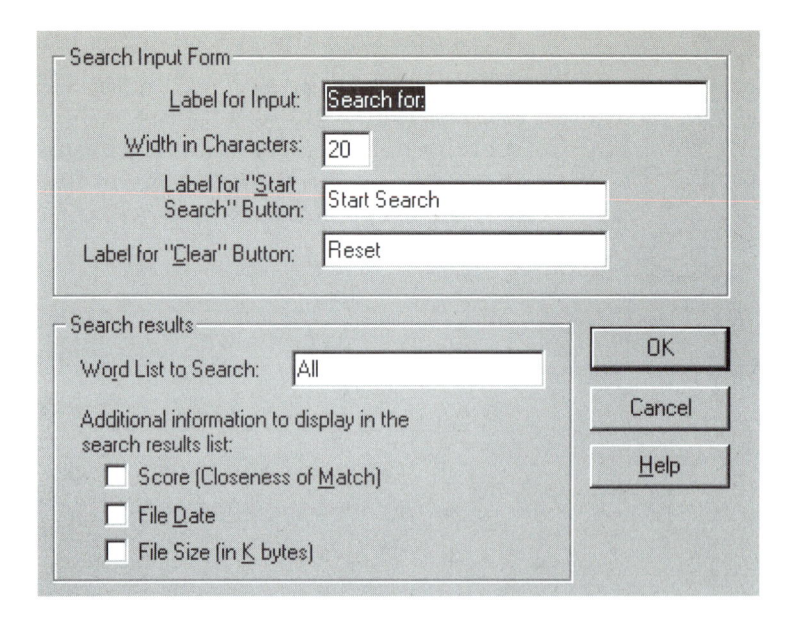

...contd

Label for Input
Enter the text that you want to use for this text box. You can input any text you wish here. The default is 'Search for'.

Width in Characters
This is the maximum number of characters that the visitor can use in a phrase to search for.

Label for "Start Search" Button
As with 'Label for Input', you can enter any text you want to appear in this button to start the search.

Label for "Clear" Button
Enter whatever text you want to appear in this button to clear the text.

Word List to Search
Enter 'All' if the search is to be across the entire site, or enter those directories that will be allowed to be searched.

Score
Indicates how closely the search matched your search.

...contd

File Date
Indicates the date and time the document that the match appears in was last modified.

File Size
Indicates the size of the file that the match appears in.

4. Click OK. FrontPage will create the WebBot and insert it in your page.

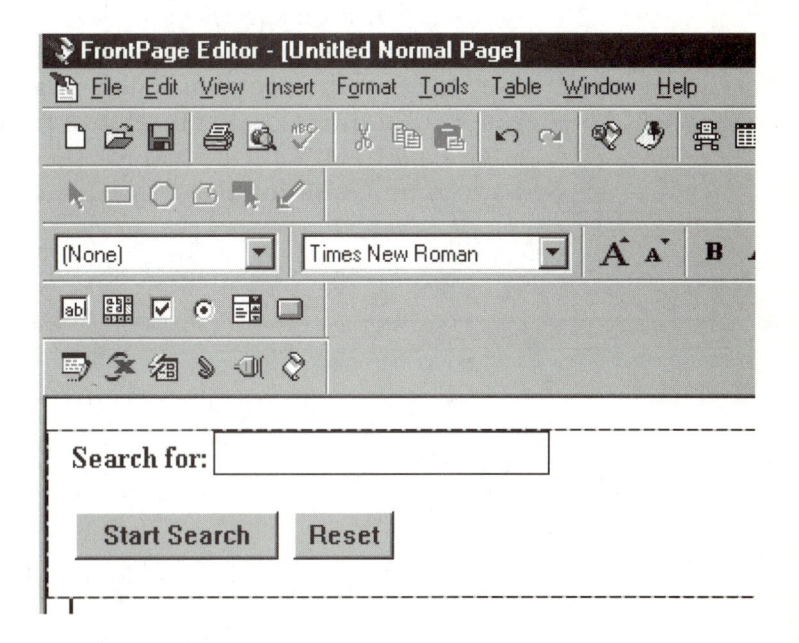

5. If you wish to change any of the entries that you made when you set up your search Bot, you can do so without creating a new one. Right-click on the WebBot component in the Editor window and choose 'Page Properties' from the pop-up menu. You will then be taken back to the Bot's setup dialogue.

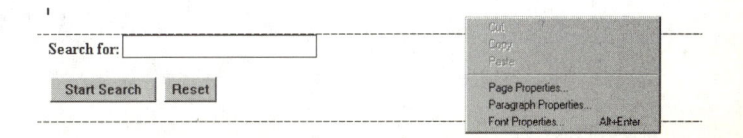

6. WebBots 107

Scheduled Image/Include WebBot

Visitors to your site will only return if there is something new for them to see or do. One of the great time-consuming activities with any Web site is updating the information on the site. Done manually, this can become a chore. There is no substitute for new content, which you should be developing as your site matures.

With the Scheduled Image and Scheduled Include WebBots, however, you can have content appear and disappear on your site at set times. You may have a new catalogue of merchandise out shortly. This can be prepared and inserted into your Web site. Using the Schedule Content Bot, the contents of this page will not appear until you want it to. Also, it will remove itself from the page after a set time. This is ideal for special offers that you only want to publicise for a short period of time.

1 Open the page on which you want to schedule the images or where you want the content to appear, and place the cursor in the right position.

2 In the Editor click on the Insert menu and then on 'WebBot Component'.

3 Highlight the 'Scheduled Include' entry and click OK.

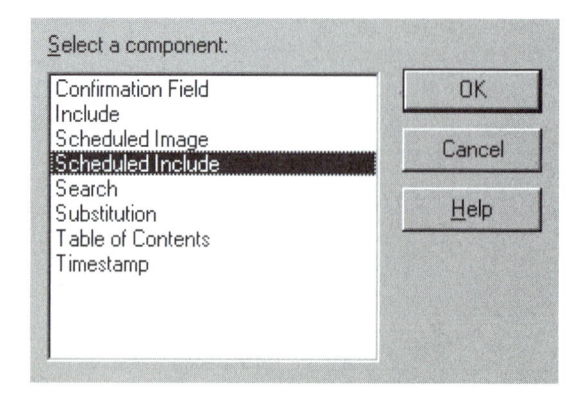

...contd

4 The properties dialogue box opens:

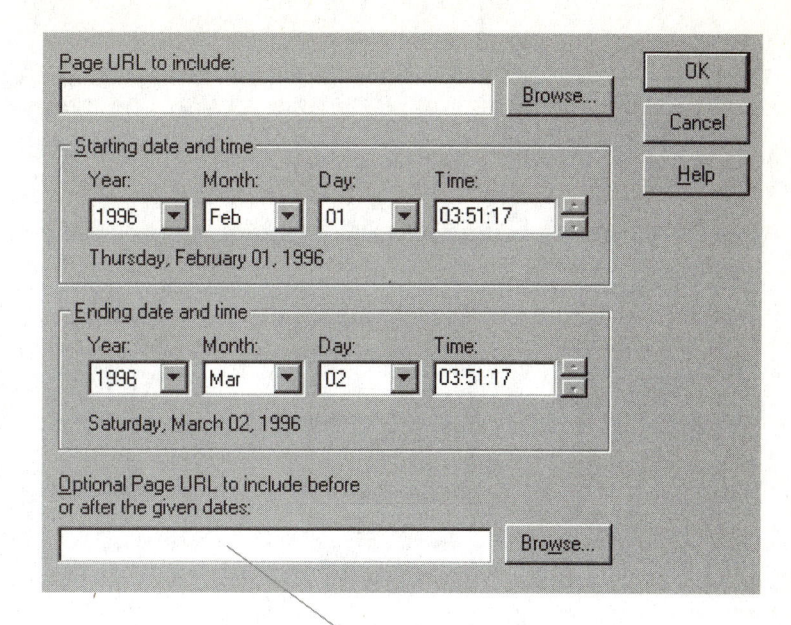

[Dialog box: Page URL to include; Starting date and time – Year: 1996, Month: Feb, Day: 01, Time: 03:51:17, Thursday, February 01, 1996; Ending date and time – Year: 1996, Month: Mar, Day: 02, Time: 03:51:17, Saturday, March 02, 1996; Optional Page URL to include before or after the given dates; OK, Cancel, Help buttons]

You can specify another image to appear in its place before and after the times you set in the rest of this dialogue box. This is a good idea, as without it your page would seem as though it had missing elements.

5 If you are within the time frame that you have entered, the image or contents will appear. If not, you will see this message appear on your page. This is for your benefit only and will not appear in the browser when the page is accessed.

[Expired Scheduled Include]

6. WebBots **109**

Substitution WebBot

The Substitution WebBot allows you to insert a variable into your pages without having to type in the information manually each time you want it to appear. You can insert this information elsewhere and then call it up and drop it into the page you are working on by using the Substitution Bot.

1. From the Editor, click on the Insert menu and then the 'WebBot Component' entry. This dialogue will open:

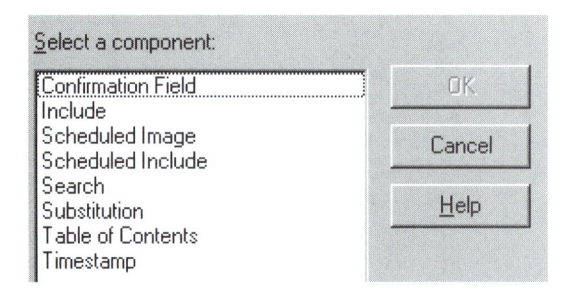

2. Double-click on the 'Substitution' WebBot entry. This dialogue will open:

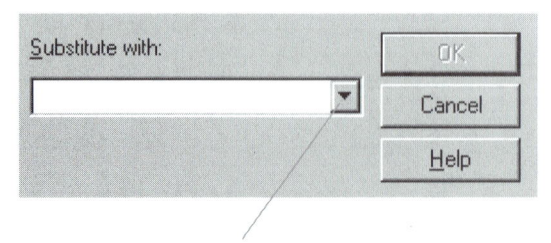

3. If you now click on this down arrow, a list of the current variables will be listed.

4. Clicking on any of these will insert that variable into the page.

FrontPage in easy steps

...contd

Adding a variable
You can add a variable to this list easily using the Web Settings command in the Explorer.

1. Open the Explorer and click on the Web Settings entry in the Tools drop-down menu.

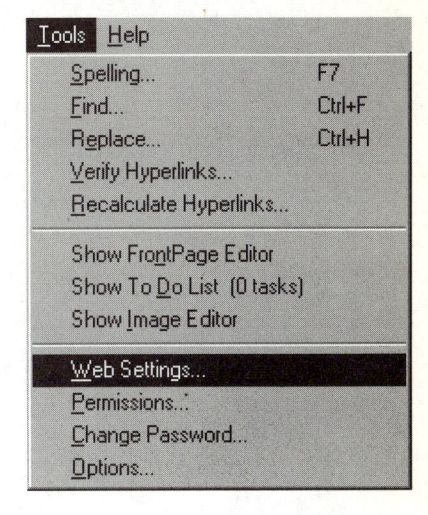

2. This dialogue will open with the Configuration tab selected. Click on the Parameters tab. You will see this screen:

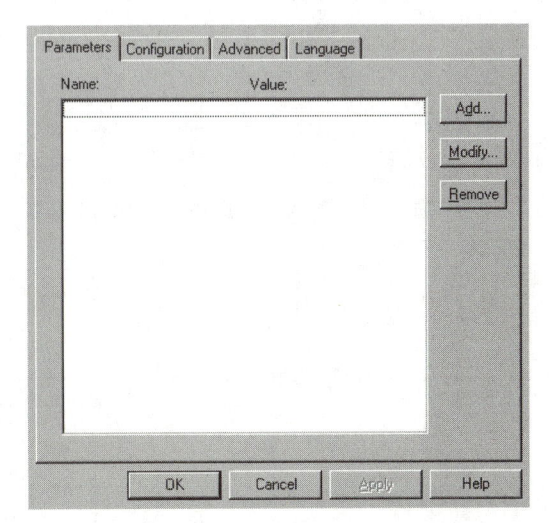

6. WebBots 111

...contd

3 Click 'Add' and this dialogue box will open. Here you enter the new variables. They can be anything you like. In this case the address and name have been used. Enter any information you want access to here and click OK.

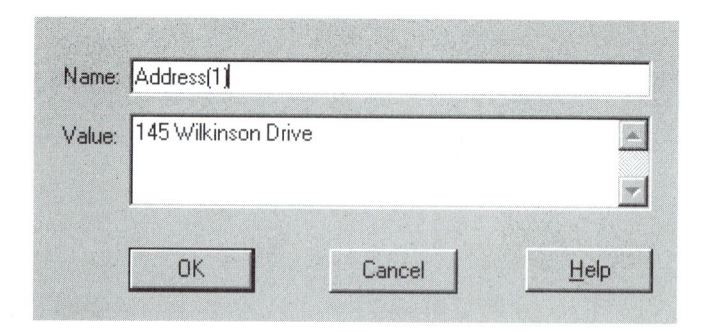

4 The new variables have been entered into the Parameters dialogue box as you see below. Now click on the 'Apply' button on the bottom of the screen. This will enter the information into memory. You can remove or modify any of the information in this screen by highlighting it and then clicking on the appropriate button.

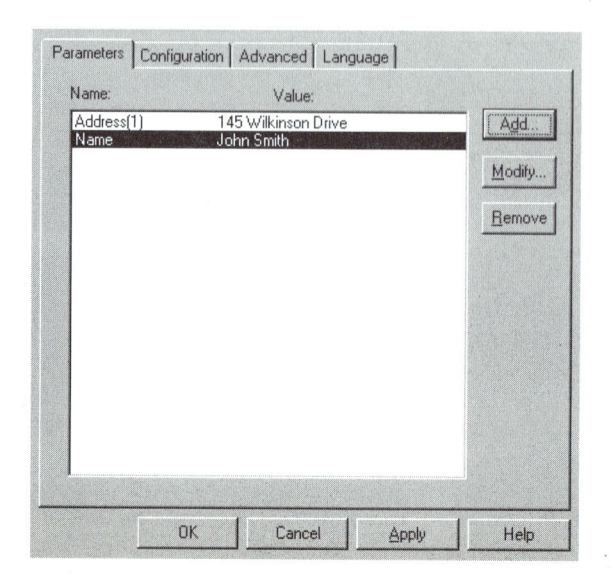

...contd

5 Now return to the Editor and open the page where you would like this information inserted.

6 Place the cursor where you would like the information to appear.

7 Open the Insert drop-down menu and click on 'WebBot Component' as you did before. You will see this screen again. Double-click on the 'Substitution' entry.

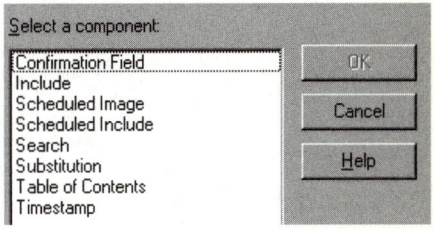

8 Click on the down arrow as in step 3. You will see the new entries of Name and Address.

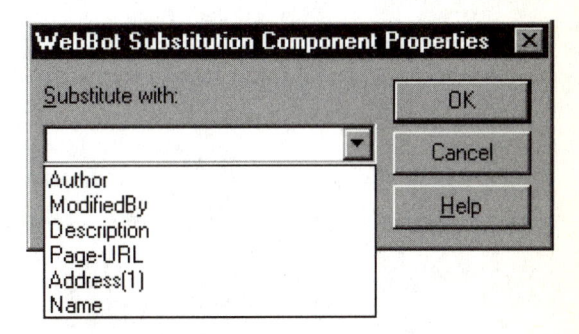

9 Double-click on one of these entries and it will be dropped into your page at the cursor point, as you see below.

145 Wilkinson Drive

6. WebBots **113**

Table of Contents WebBot

FrontPage allows you to create those elements on your site that have in the past been time-consuming and tedious. One of these has been the creation of a table of contents for your site. FrontPage comes with a WebBot that automates this process.

1. Open the Editor and load the page where you would like the table of contents to be inserted. Place the cursor where you want the table to appear.

2. From the Insert menu, select the 'WebBot Component' entry.

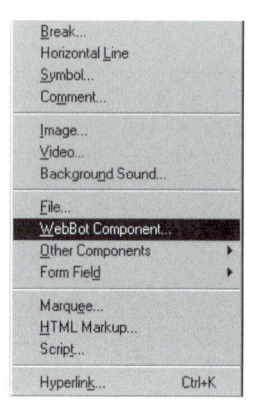

3. This now familiar dialogue box appears. Select the 'Table of Contents' entry and click OK, or double-click on the entry.

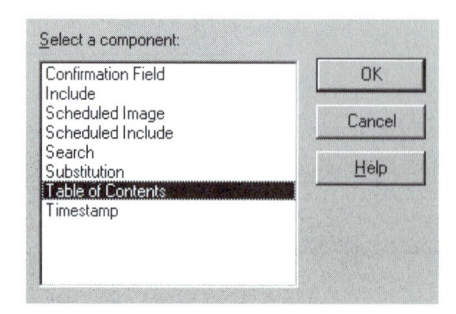

FrontPage in easy steps

...contd

HANDY TIP

If you want to compile a complete contents of your site, enter the URL of your Home page.

4 This is the properties dialogue box:

Enter the URL that you want the table of contents to begin with. It will include all the links to that page.

If a page has multiple links to this page, it will appear in the contents page more than once if you do not tick this box.

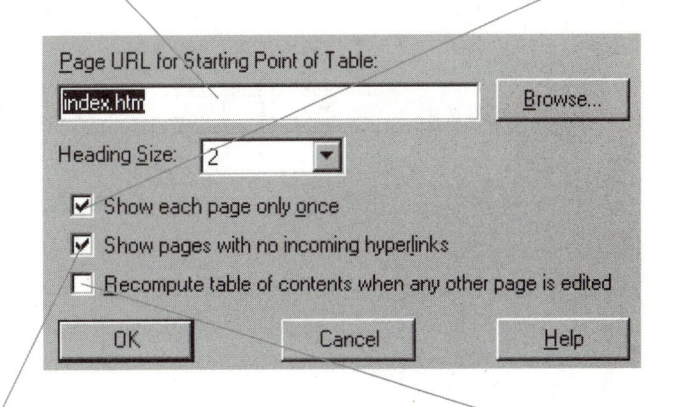

If you have pages that have no links at all to any other page, ticking this box will still allow them to be shown in the table of contents.

Tick this box so that the table of contents is recomputed each time you make a change to a Web page on your site.

5 You set the Heading style from this drop-down menu. If you don't want any style applied to your headings, enter 0.

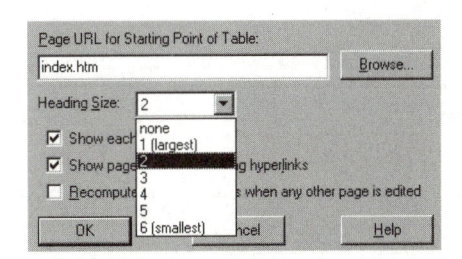

6. WebBots **115**

...contd

6 When you have set all of the parameters in the properties dialogue box, click OK and the WebBot will create the contents entry for you:

Table of Contents Heading Page

- Title of a Page
- Title of a Page
- Title of a Page

Timestamp WebBot

Return visitors to your site will want to know if it has been updated recently, and therefore if it is worth their while to stay at your site and look around. One of the easiest ways of doing this is to date-stamp your pages. This is easily set up with the Timestamp Bot.

1   Open the Editor and load the page where you would like the time-stamp to be inserted. Place the cursor where you want the time-stamp to appear.

2   Drop down the Insert menu and click on the WebBot Component entry. You will see this familiar dialogue box:

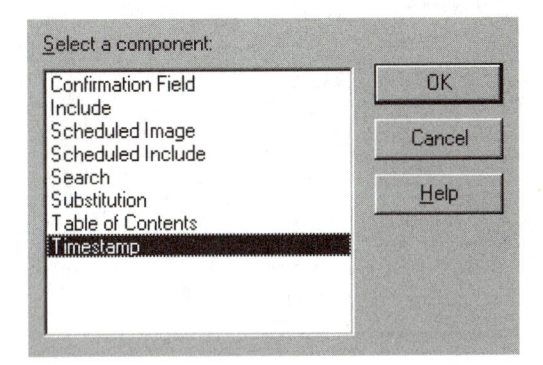

3   Select the 'Timestamp' entry and click OK, or double-click on the entry.

4   This is the properties dialogue box. Choose to have the date reflect the last time the page was updated or the last time it was edited. For a full explanation of these, see the next page.

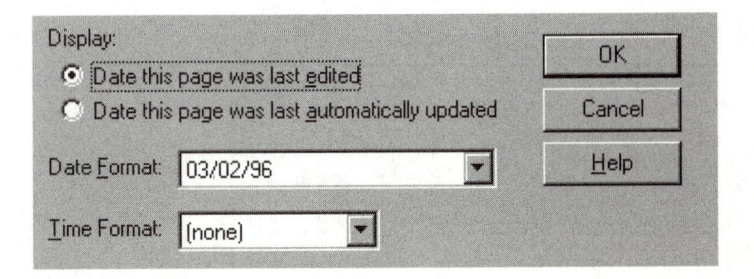

6. WebBots 117

...contd

5 This is the Timestamp Component Properties dialogue, with the Date Format drop-down menu. Choose a date format you want to use and click OK. The date will be inserted at the cursor point.

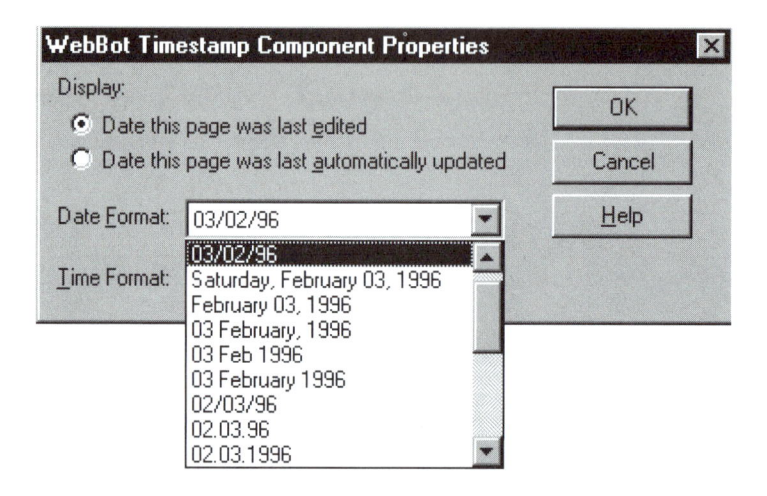

6 Here the date and time have been inserted. Also you can add some text before or after the date and time as you wish.

Last modified:Saturday, February 03, 1996 12:29

Edited
Your page is 'Edited' when it has been changed in some way and has been saved to the server.

Updated
Your page is 'Updated' when the actual HTML code it is based on has been generated. It does not necessarily mean that you have to save the page to the server, however.

Registration WebBot

As you have surfed the Internet you will have come across some sites that only allow access to the whole site or a specific part of it via a registration form. Many of the large publishing houses use this technique to add your details to their database for marketing purposes. This WebBot allows you to do the same thing with your whole Web site, or just a few selected pages.

Finding out who is visiting your site is an important means of reaching new customers if you are selling goods or a service. You may also have a certain area of your Web site to which you would only like to offer access to certain visitors. Perhaps you have created a privileged club for some of your customers, and only those who register can look at these selected pages. FrontPage allows you to set this up with the least amount of fuss.

1   From the Editor, select 'New' from the File menu. You will see this now familiar dialogue box open. Double-click on 'User Registration'.

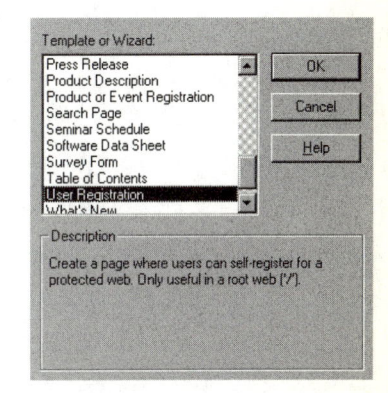

2   You will see the form (shown on p.120) open. You also have full control over the settings that are contained in the WebBot handler that you need to choose to work with this WebBot. To open the properties dialogue box, right-click on the form and select 'Form Properties' from the pop-up menu.

...contd

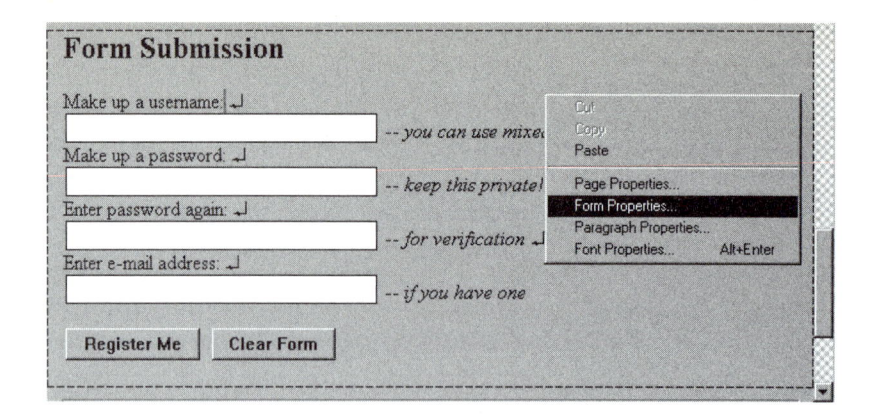

3   From this dialogue box you configure the handler that will be used with the form. For more details on this dialogue box, see Chapter Seven. On pages 135-138, you will see how you set up a handler for the particular form you have created.

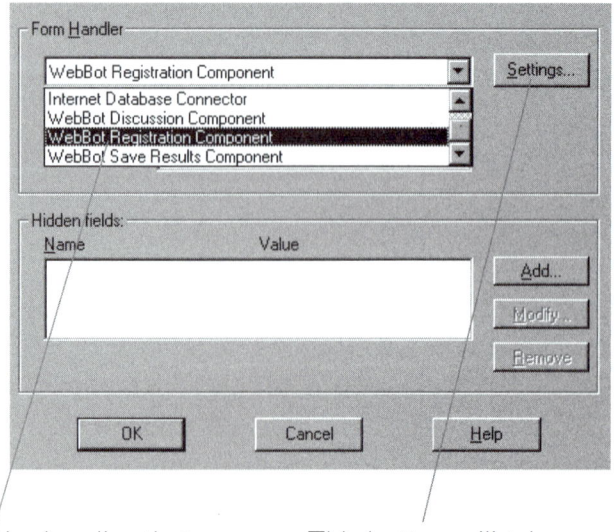

Choose the handler that suits the WebBot and type of form you have created.

This button will take you to the configuration dialogue box.

CHAPTER SEVEN

Forms and Fields

Forms are one of the most useful means of communicating with the visitors to your site. You can gain valuable information about who is accessing your site and provide feedback to your visitors or customers.

FrontPage automates the creation of forms to some extent. In this chapter you will see how you can add a form field to a template or even a Wizard that you have already created. Also, you will learn how to set up the Bots you will need to collect the information that your visitors are sending.

Covers

Form Page Wizard	122
Form Fields	127
Field Types	129
Field Validation	131
Form Properties	135
Configuring a Handler	137

Form Page Wizard

You are bound to have come across forms when you have been surfing the Internet. You will have filled some in yourself to ask for information, to register with a site or to take part in a discussion. FrontPage allows you to create these forms easily, and modify them to your own specific needs. With the Form Page Wizard you can create just about any kind of form you like.

Later in this chapter you will see how you can add to these forms by inserting your own fields; and finally how these will relate to your Web site as a whole and the server you will be using.

1 Open the Editor, drop down the File menu and click on 'New'.

2 This dialogue will open. Choose 'Form Page Wizard' and click OK.

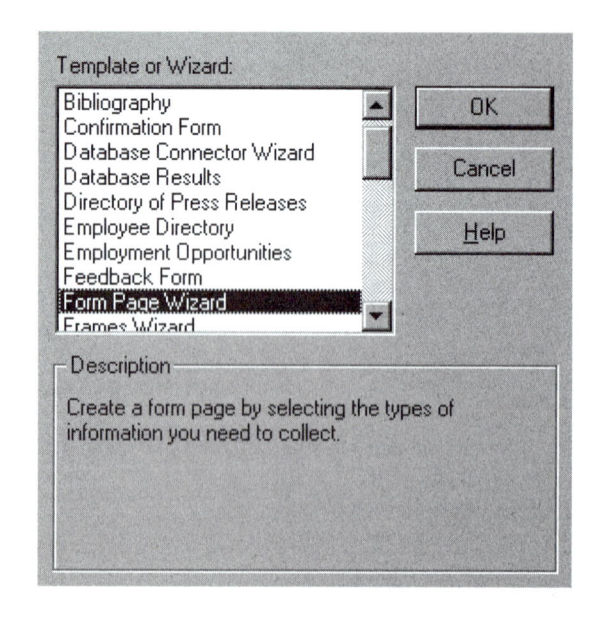

This dialogue box should be familiar as you saw it first in Chapter Four, 'Wizards and Templates'.

...contd

3 This is the opening screen of the Form Page Wizard.

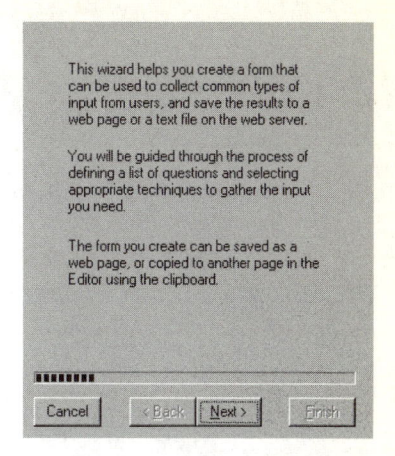

REMEMBER

File names can only be eight characters long, plus the htm extension.

4 Enter the file name of the page and its title. Click Next when you have finished.

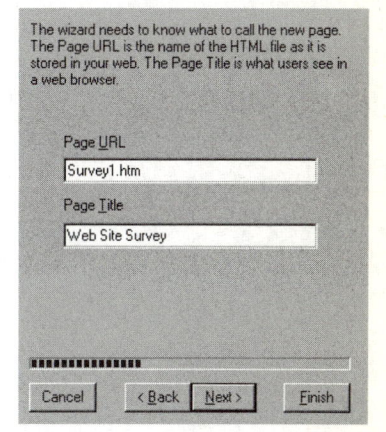

5 This is where you enter the questions you want to ask on your form. Clicking 'Add' will take you to the next screen.

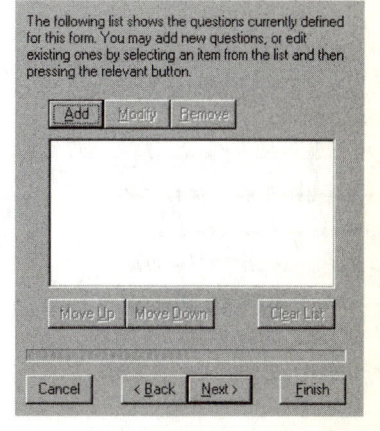

7. Forms and Fields **123**

...contd

6 Choose a category that is appropriate to the form that you are designing. In this case, personal information is being collected.

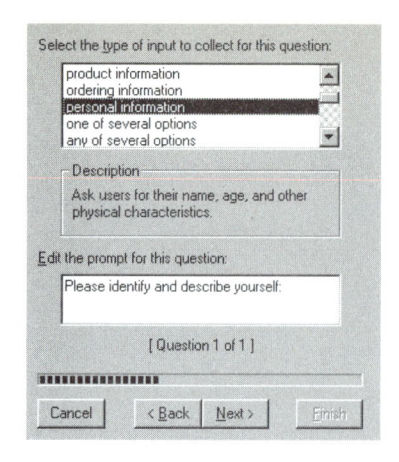

7 Choose from this selection of questions what you would like to appear on the form. Click 'Next' when you are finished.

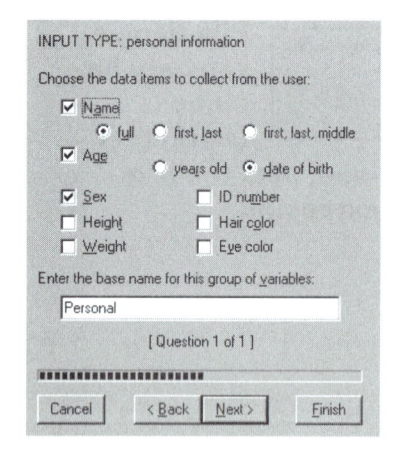

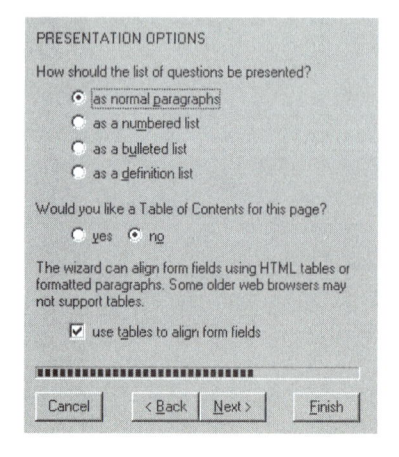

REMEMBER

If you ask for a Table of Contents on this screen, you will have to edit this manually on the page to show what questions are being asked on the form.

8 Enter how you would like your questions presented and click 'Next'.

124 FrontPage in easy steps

...contd

9 After the screen in step 8, you will be returned to this screen which you saw in step 5. Now that you have your questions entered you can modify them, or remove them from your form. If you click on a question in the large window, the Modify and Remove buttons will become active.

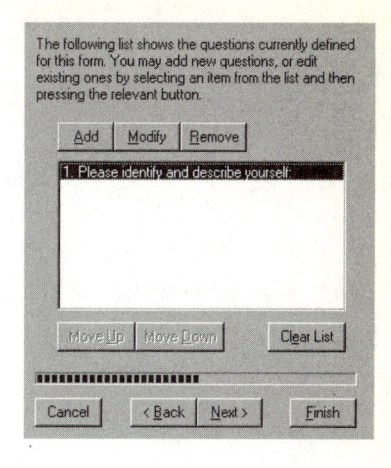

10 This screen allows you to choose how the information from the form will be stored. Click on one button.

If the server that you are going to use doesn't have the FrontPage Server Extensions, you will not be able to process the form using a FrontPage Bot. In this case you can assign a CGI script to process these forms on the server.

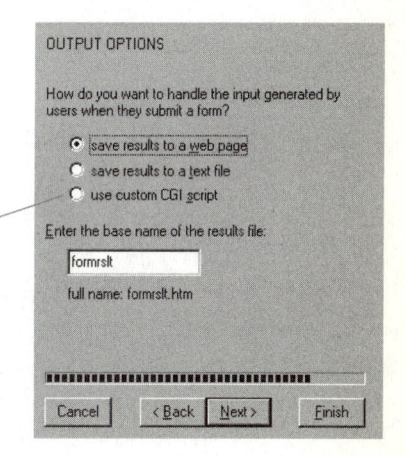

7. Forms and Fields

...contd

11 This is the last screen you will see when using this Wizard. It tells you that you have answered all the questions that it needs to create the form you have designed. Click Finish and the form will be created in the Editor.

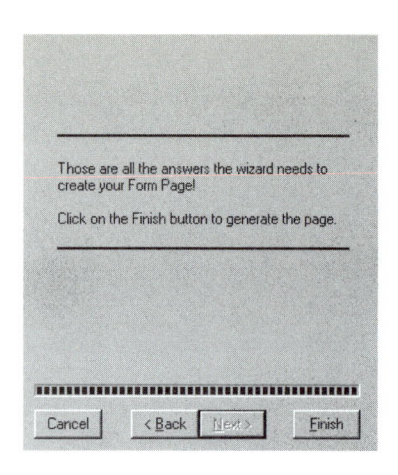

12 Here is the completed form open in the Editor. You can see the fields that go up to make the form. These are the boxes that your visitors type their answers into. Next in this chapter you will see how you can add fields to any form that you have created to customise it to your exact needs.

126 FrontPage in easy steps

Form Fields

As an example of a form we will create a feedback form, as this shows all of the types of field that can be used in a form in FrontPage. As always, FrontPage provides a quick and easy route to creating what can be quite complex forms.

1   Open the Editor, drop down the File menu and click on New.

2   This dialogue will open. Choose 'Feedback Form' from the list and click OK.

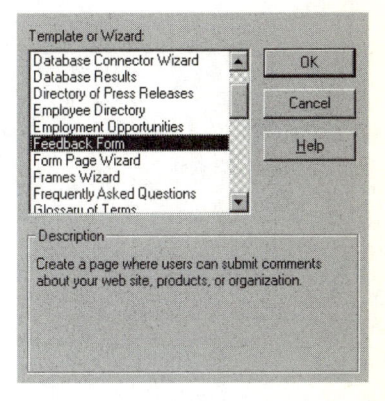

3   This is a section of the feedback form that is created in the Editor.

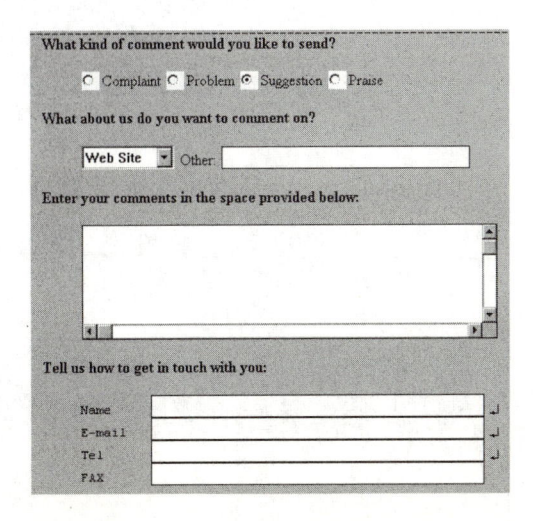

7. Forms and Fields   **127**

...contd

The example overleaf is the feedback form that can be created automatically with a FrontPage Template. It does however show you all of the types of fields that you can include in a form, or any other document. The different types of fields are listed in this section.

1. There are two ways in which you can insert a field into your Web pages. From the drop-down menu, open the Editor and go to the Insert menu. You will see the entry 'Form Field'. This is a cascading menu. If you move your mouse pointer to the arrow, you will see all of the available fields listed.

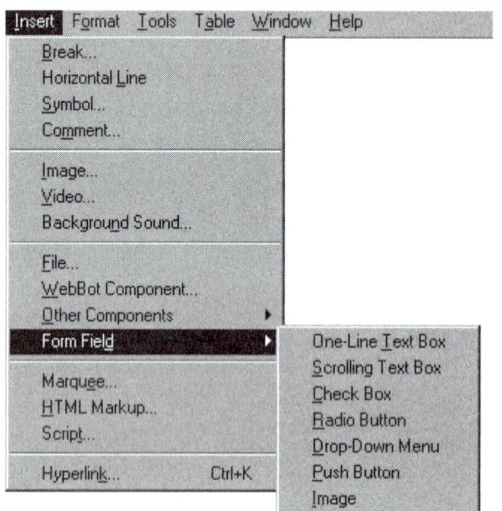

2. The alternative is to use the icons in the toolbar. If you cannot see the icons shown below, go to the View menu and click on 'Forms Toolbar'.

Field Types

There are six field types that you can choose from. They are all listed below with a screenshot of how they look when they are inserted into a Web page. Also shown is the icon that you can click on to insert the field into your page. These are shown for easy reference.

REMEMBER *In this field the number of characters that can be typed is set by the overall size of the box. This cannot be exceeded.*

One-Line Text Box

Visitors can type in this box. You set this in the properties dialogue box.

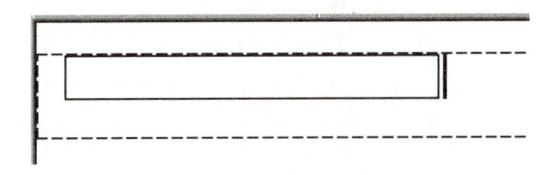

Scrolling Text Box

This is usually supplied on your Web page so your visitors can write lengthy messages to you if they want to, or if you have asked for a lengthy answer to a question.

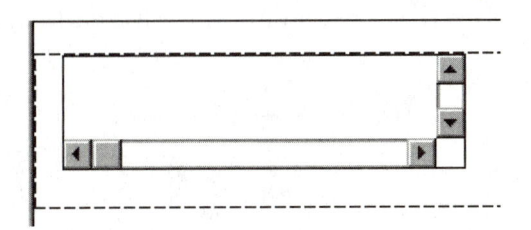

Check Box

As its name suggests, a tick or check will appear in it when the mouse is clicked on it. These are used when you ask a question and want a 'yes' or 'no' answer.

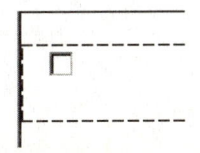

7. Forms and Fields

...contd

Radio Button

These can be used with a list of items where you only want the visitor to select one option.

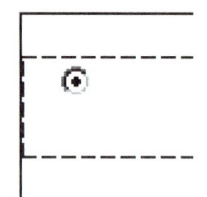

Drop-Down Menu

These allow the visitor to choose one or more items from a list.

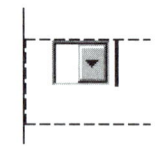

Push Button

Can be used to submit the information that has just been entered into the form, or to clear the form and start again.

Field Validation

For each field there is a Validation dialogue box. Here you set how the field will behave when data is entered into it. As an example, the scrolling text box field has been used here. You will see how with FrontPage you have total control over how the field behaves when it is accessed by the browser of your visitor.

1   Open the Editor to a blank page and insert a Scrolling text Box at a cursor point. You can click on the icon in the toolbar or use the Insert menu.

2   You will see this field inserted on the Web page. Highlight it by left-clicking on it. You will see small squares appear at each corner to show that it has been done.

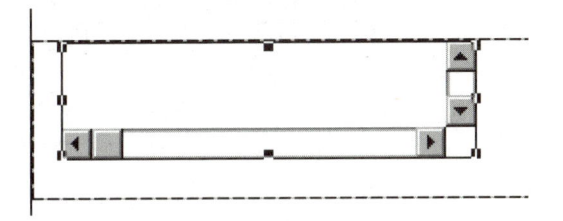

3   If you right-click on the field, this menu will pop-up. Click on the 'Form Field Validation' entry.

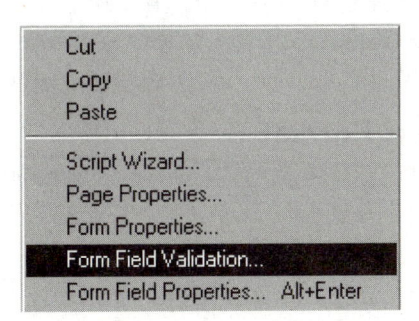

7. Forms and Fields   **131**

...contd

4 The Text Box Validation dialogue is displayed. From here the settings of the scrolling text box are entered.

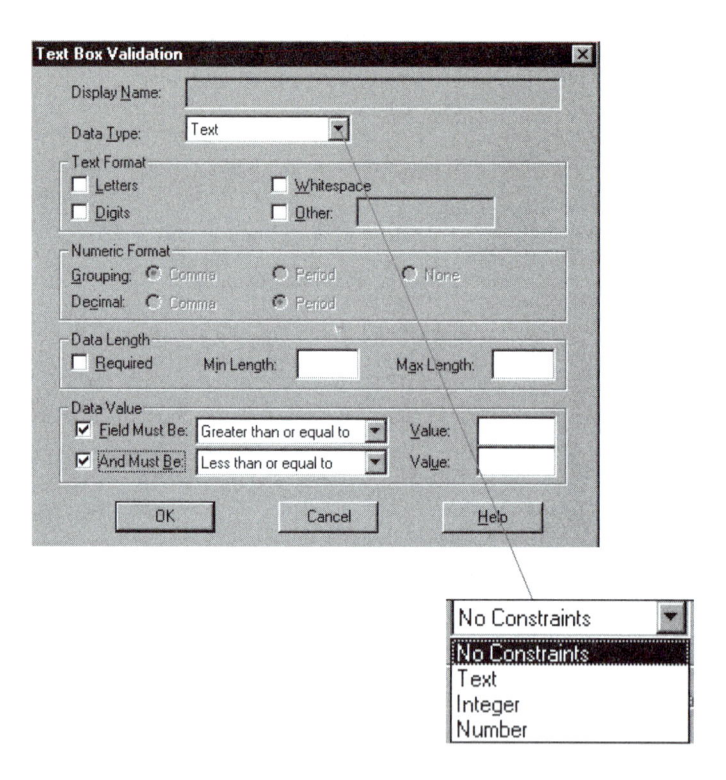

Display Name
This is the name that the field is given on the page. Sometimes the label that is typed onto the page directly doesn't match the internal name of the field. In this case, type the field name into this space.

Text Format
The available settings for these sections are determined by the active entry in the Data Type drop-down menu.

Letters
Indicates that the field can only contain text.

Digits
Indicates that the field can only contain numeric characters.

...contd

Whitespace
Indicates that the field can contain white space such as line feeds or carriage returns.

Other
Indicates that the field can contain other characters such as commas or hyphens.

Numeric Format

Grouping
This specifies what kind of punctuation is allowed with numbers.

None: Indicates that no punctuation is allowed. E.g.: 1234567890

Comma: Indicates that the comma is allowed. E.g.: 1,234,567,890

Full stop: Indicates that the full stop is allowed. E.g.: 1.234.567.890

Decimal
You can specify a character to use as a decimal point.

Full stop: E.g.: 123.4567890

Comma: E.g.: 123,4567890

Data Length
This section allows you to set the data length of any data type.

Required
Activate this feature to show that data is required in this field.

Min Length/Max Length
Specify the maximum and minimum data length.

7. Forms and Fields **133**

...contd

Data Value
This section is for setting the values for any type of data.

Field Must Be
Click on the down arrow and choose an appropriate value for your field. For instance, if you are using numerical data, you might choose 'Greater than or equal to' here.

Value
To complete the data value you must set a value that matches your last choice. For instance, if you enter 50 here, this specifies that the data that is inputted must be greater than or equal to 50.

And Must Be
As in the previous example, choose the data constraint from the drop-down list and then type in a second data constraint.

You will find a Validation dialogue for each of the field types, although they are not all as complex as this one. Like the one above, you have a number of options that you can set to give the field the properties you want it to have.

Form Properties

You have seen how you can create your own forms from a number of fields. You can create a form from scratch or use one of the templates supplied and add your own touches.

You have already seen how you can set up the form using the Form Properties dialogue box. You must now set the Form Handler. These are like glue that binds the form you have created to your server. The Handler is part of the FrontPage Server and is really just a specialised WebBot. It takes the information that your visitors have inputted into the form and saves it in some way, then passes it on to you.

1 Open the form that you have created and highlight one of the fields. Right-click on it and you will see this menu open. Click on the 'Form Properties' entry.

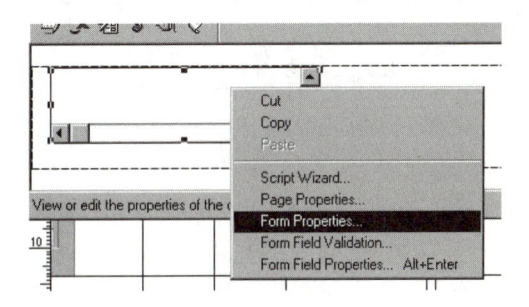

2 This is the main Form Properties dialogue box:

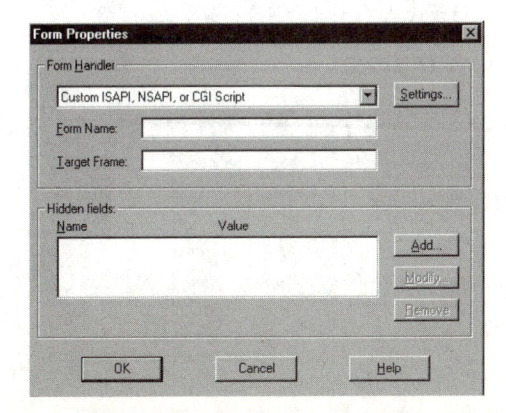

7. Forms and Fields **135**

...contd

3 If you click the down arrow in the Form Properties dialogue box you will see all of the handlers that are available to use with your form.

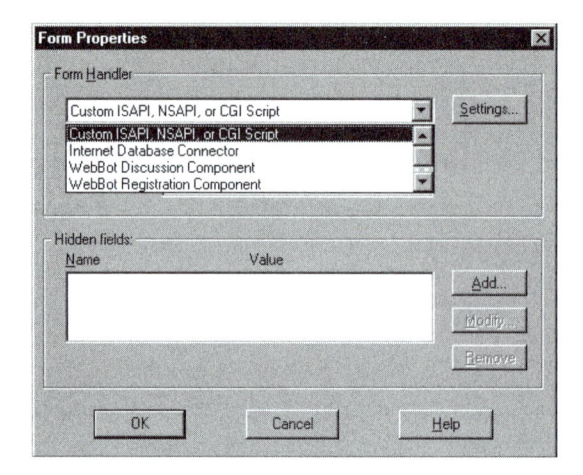

4 From the menu, choose the type of handler that best suits your form.

5 Since we used the feedback form as an example, choose 'WebBot Save Results Component' from the list, then click OK.

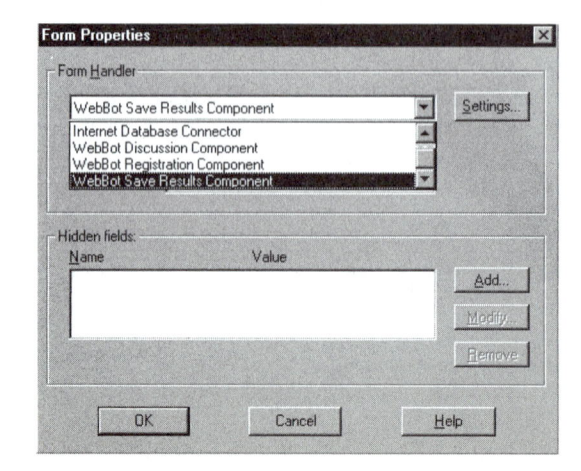

Configuring a Handler

To set up the Handler for your form, open the form and the Form Properties dialogue box as you did in the last section. You will see a Settings button at the top right-hand corner of the dialogue box. Click on it now. You will see this dialogue open.

1 Type the name of the file containing the results and its location on the server.

2 Click on the down arrow on the File Format entry and you will see a drop-down list to choose from:

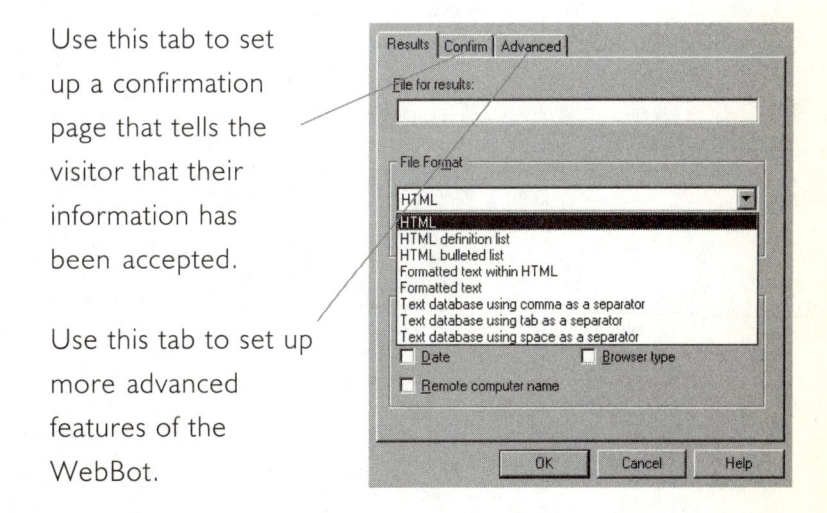

Use this tab to set up a confirmation page that tells the visitor that their information has been accepted.

Use this tab to set up more advanced features of the WebBot.

7. Forms and Fields   137

...contd

The drop-down list that you see when you click the down arrow gives you a number of options regarding the file format in which the information you are gathering will be presented.

HTML
Formats the text as standard HTML code.

HTML definition list
These are often used to add dictionaries to FrontPage Webs.

HTML bulleted list
Formats the file using a bulleted list for the entries.

Formatted text within HTML
Formats the text with line endings.

Formatted text
Formats the text in an easy-to-read layout.

Text database using comma as a separator
Separates the information with commas. Useful if the information is going to be used with a database.

Text database using tab as a separator
Formats the text in the same way as above, but uses tabs instead of commas. Useful if the information is used in a spreadsheet.

Text database using space as a separator
Formats the text in the same way as above, but uses spaces instead of commas or tabs. Useful if the information is used in a spreadsheet.

CHAPTER EIGHT

The Personal Web Server

This last chapter deals with the server that your Web pages will be accessed from. Server software is supplied with FrontPage so you can test your web site before it goes live. It is a full 32-bit server and can be used as a low volume server on a small Intranet. This chapter will cover the server itself and also your ISP (Internet Service Provider), and going live with your site.

Covers

The Personal Web Server	140
Server Extensions	141
The Server Administrator	142
Publishing Your Web Site	145
Publish FrontPage Web	145
FTP	148
FrontPage Publishing Wizard	149

The Personal Web Server

As you approach the completion of your Web site, you will need to test it before you give full access to its pages. The Personal Web Server allows just this. On one single computer you can test all of your pages, their links and WebBots to make sure all are working as you want them to.

This is really all you will see of the Server itself. It doesn't need any setting up; it is set up when you install FrontPage for the first time. The Server fully supports CGI (Common Gateway Interface) scripts and HTTP (Hypertext Transfer Protocol), and is based on the NCSA (National Centre for Supercomputing Applications) standards. If you haven't seen this screen before, look at the bottom of your monitor. It should be minimised there, and be running when you are working with FrontPage.

Server Extensions

Server Extensions allow you to connect your Web site to the World Wide Web via the server of your choice. They provide the communications between the client – the computer of the user who wants to look at your site, and the Server – the computer that the Web site is stored on.

When you installed FrontPage, its Server Extensions were installed at the same time. If, however, you want to run your Web site from a different computer you must first install the Server Extensions for it, and use the Server Administrator to link your pages to the server it is running on.

FrontPage supports a large number of computer platforms and has Server Extensions for the majority of them. A full list is kept on the Microsoft Web site: Look at

```
http://www.microsoft.com/frontpage
```

Look for the Server Extensions you need and download them. Then follow the instructions for installing them on your particular computer.

For example, Server Extensions are available for:

Platforms
- Windows 95
- Windows NT (Workstation and Server versions)
- UNIX

Commercial Web Servers
- Netscape Communications
- Microsoft Internet Information Server

Non-commercial Web Servers
- CERN
- NCSA
- Apache

The Server Administrator

The Server Administrator is a small program that allows you to carry out tasks that relate to the Server side of FrontPage. Amongst many other things, this program allows you to upgrade your software, change passwords and uninstall the FrontPage Server Extensions if you need to.

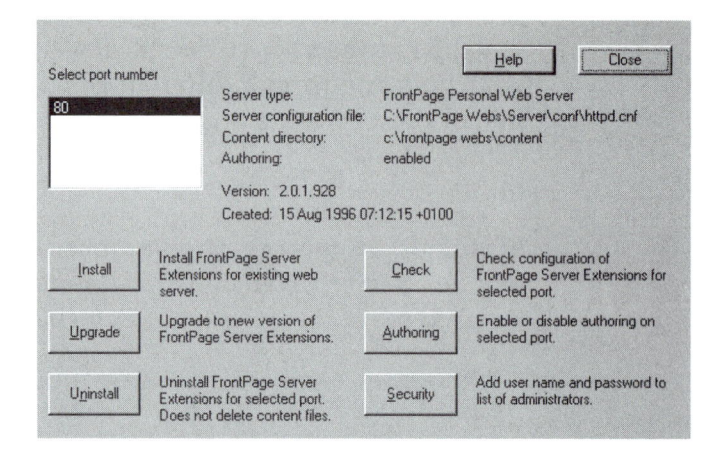

Install

Taking each one of the above buttons in turn, the first is used to install the FrontPage Server Extensions.

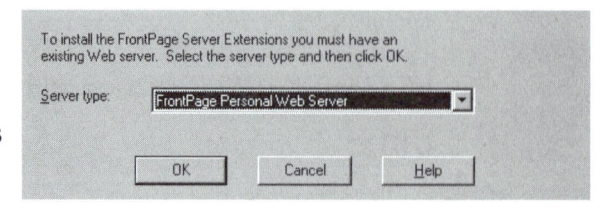

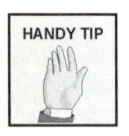

HANDY TIP — It is always a good idea to test the server you are going to use with a browser before you install any extensions, to make sure it is operating properly.

If you click on the down arrow you will see all of the available Servers. Before you can install a set of Server Extensions, you need to have a server running on your system. Choose the one you would like to use the extensions with.

...contd

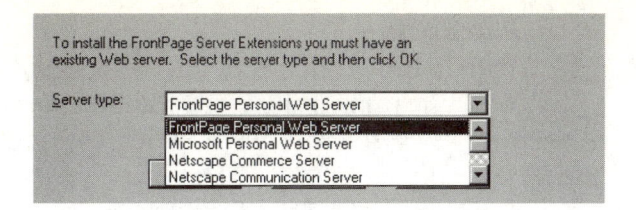

Choose from this list of Servers the one you want to install extensions with. Then click OK.

Uninstall

If you uninstall an extension by clicking on this button, FrontPage will confirm with this dialogue what will be deleted. You can then decide if you want to proceed.

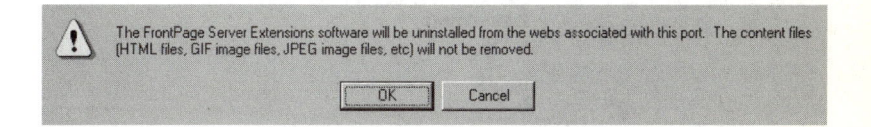

Check

As the button states, this function checks the Server Extensions against the selected port number. If all is well you will see this dialogue box pop up. Click OK to return to the main screen.

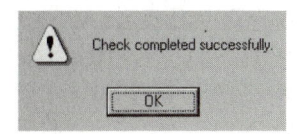

...contd

Authoring

This is linked in a way to the security you can apply to your Web sites. From here you can decide who gains access to your Web site and from which computers.

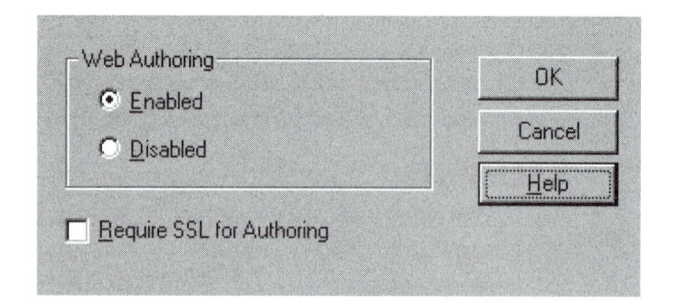

Enabled
Select this option to allow Web authoring on the stated port.

Disabled
Select this option to disallow Web authoring on this port. When this is selected, FrontPage will not be able to access the Webs on this port.

Require SSL for Authoring
When this option is selected, the FrontPage Server Extension will verify whether this option has been activated when it comes to publish your Web pages. The server must be set up to support SSL (Secure Socket Layer) authoring before you publish your Web site.

Publishing Your Web Site

If you are planning on using someone else's server to house your Web site, you need to publish it to that server. There are three ways in which you can do this; which one you use will depend on whether or not the server has the FrontPage Server Extensions installed. Check with your ISP (Internet Service Provider) before you attempt to copy any files to their server.

The three methods of publishing are as follows:

- Publish FrontPage Web
- FTP (File Transfer Protocol)
- FrontPage Publishing Wizard

Publish FrontPage Web

This way of transferring your Web pages to the server is only available if the server has the FrontPage Server Extensions installed. This is the simplest way of transferring your site, as it is built into FrontPage itself.

After you have made a connection with your ISP (Internet Service Provider), open the Explorer. Drop down the File menu and click on 'Publish FrontPage Web'.

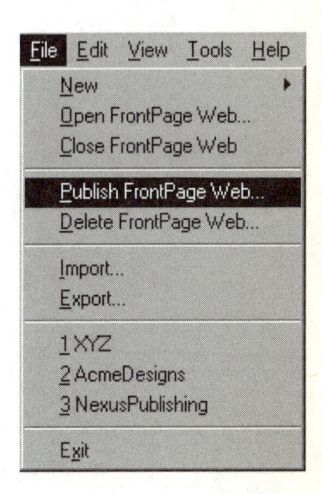

...contd

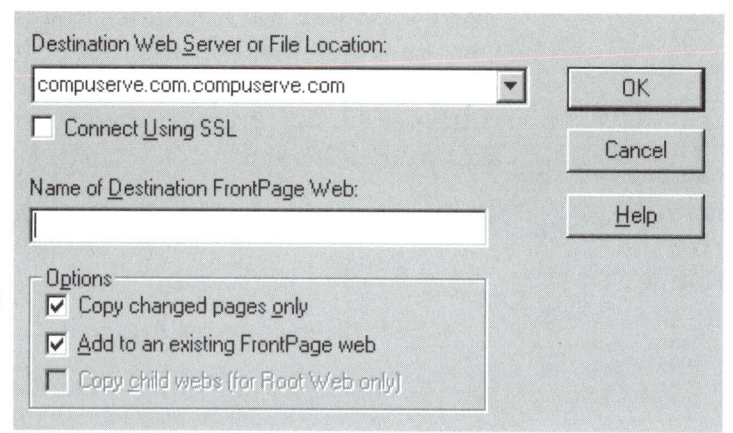

BEWARE

The copying of your files may take some time. If your server 'times you out' after a set amount of time, it may assume that the connection has been broken and drop the line. If you have this problem when you copy your Web to its final server, you will have to talk to your ISP about this.

2 This dialogue box will open:

3 In the first Destination Web Server or File Location box, enter the server name or IP address.

4 In the Name of Destination FrontPage Web box, enter the name of the Web you want to copy to the server.

5 **Connect Using SSL**

SSL or Secure Sockets Layer is a means of connecting to your server and transferring your Web in a secure environment. Many companies use this technology to transfer such things as credit card numbers. If the server supports SSL, click on this box.

6 **Options:**

Copy Changed Pages Only

Click on this box if you are republishing to an existing Web site. FrontPage will only copy those files that have changed since the site was last copied.

...contd

BEWARE

If you use the 'Add to an existing FrontPage web' command in the Options section, the new files will overwrite the existing ones on the server if they have the same name.

Add to Existing FrontPage Web

You should use this option if you want to add your Web pages to a site that already exists.

Copy Child Webs

This option copies Web pages that are part of the Root Web.

As you are copying your Web site to a remote server, you will be asked to provide a password. This you enter in the familiar Web name and password dialogue box.

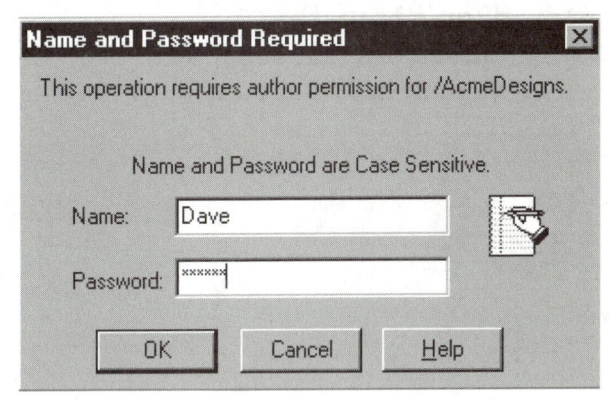

If all goes well, FrontPage will publish the pages that you have specified. You will then see a dialogue box pop up to confirm this.

> The AcmeDesigns web has been successfully copied to: http://compuserve.com.compuserve.com/.

8. The Personal Web Server **147**

FTP

If you decide that you want to use FTP to transfer your files to your server, there are a few points to bear in mind as you decide what to transfer and what to leave on your computer. Mostly they have to do with the FrontPage Server Extensions, and whether or not the server you are going to use supports them or not.

Transfer

All the files that your Root Web contains. These include all Child Web directories and their subdirectories.

All images that are contained in the Images subdirectory.

Don't transfer

Directories that begin with _vti. These are files that contain information about FrontPage Extensions.

FrontPage Publishing Wizard

In keeping with the ease of use of FrontPage, if you discover that your ISP's server doesn't have the FrontPage Server Extensions installed on it, you can still publish your finished Web page to that server. You won't be able to use the WebBots that you may have incorporated in some of your pages, but the Publishing Wizard will make the whole process straightforward.

If you don't know if you installed the FrontPage Publishing Wizard when you installed FrontPage itself from the CD, you can check by inserting the CD into your computer again. It will auto-run and you will see this screen once again. As you can see, you are told which programs have been installed and which haven't. If you hadn't installed the Publishing Wizard, do this now by clicking on the icon.

You may think that this way of publishing your Web site to your server is very similar to FTP. You would be correct, but the Publishing Wizard offers a more user friendly approach to this task. Also, you will not have to manually select the files you need to copy. You can also tell the Wizard only to publish those pages that have changed since the last time you published the Web site.

8. The Personal Web Server

...contd

When you have installed the Publishing Wizard you can access it through the Start menu on your desktop.

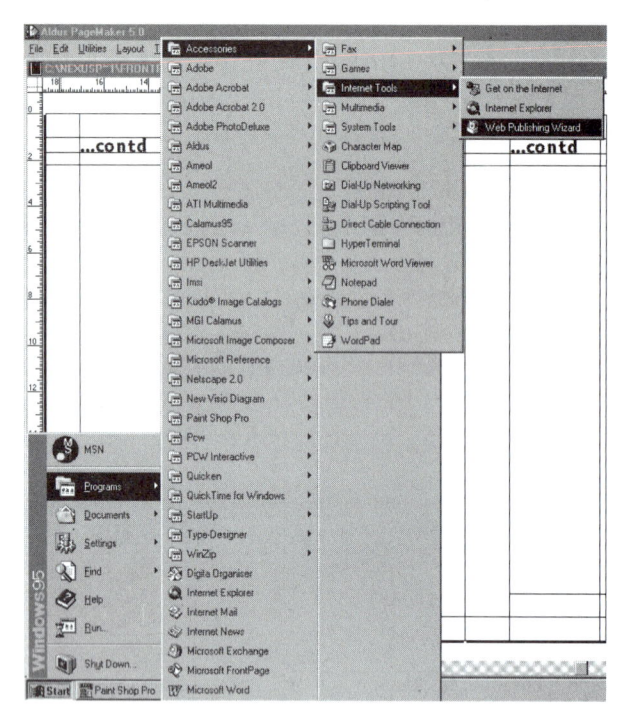

HANDY TIP **You can set up your server access at this point. Windows users are however advised to install their connection before using this Wizard. This will make the whole process much easier and more straightforward.**

Before you start the Publishing Wizard you will need to set up your Internet connection and the server where your Web site will be accessed from. You will need the full URL of the server and have your user name and password ready to enter into the Wizard. If you haven't installed your Internet connection software and set up your account, do this now. The Publishing Wizard will not do this for you.

For this example, a connection to CompuServe will be shown. You will see slightly different screens for other service providers. They will all give you access information that you will need when using this Wizard.

| Make your connection to the server to which you will be copying your Web site.

...contd

2 Start the Publishing Wizard. You will see this opening screen:

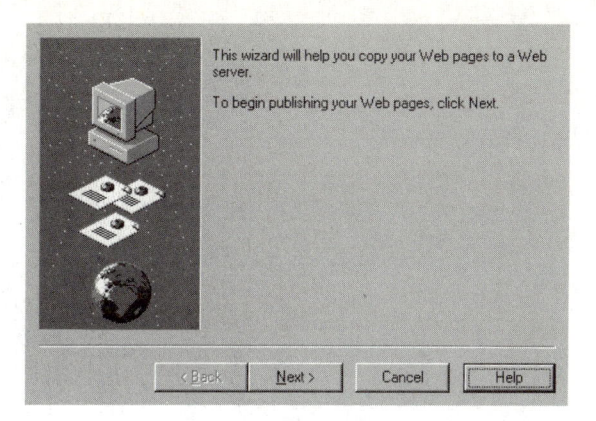

3 Enter the file name or folder name and path of the Web you want to publish.

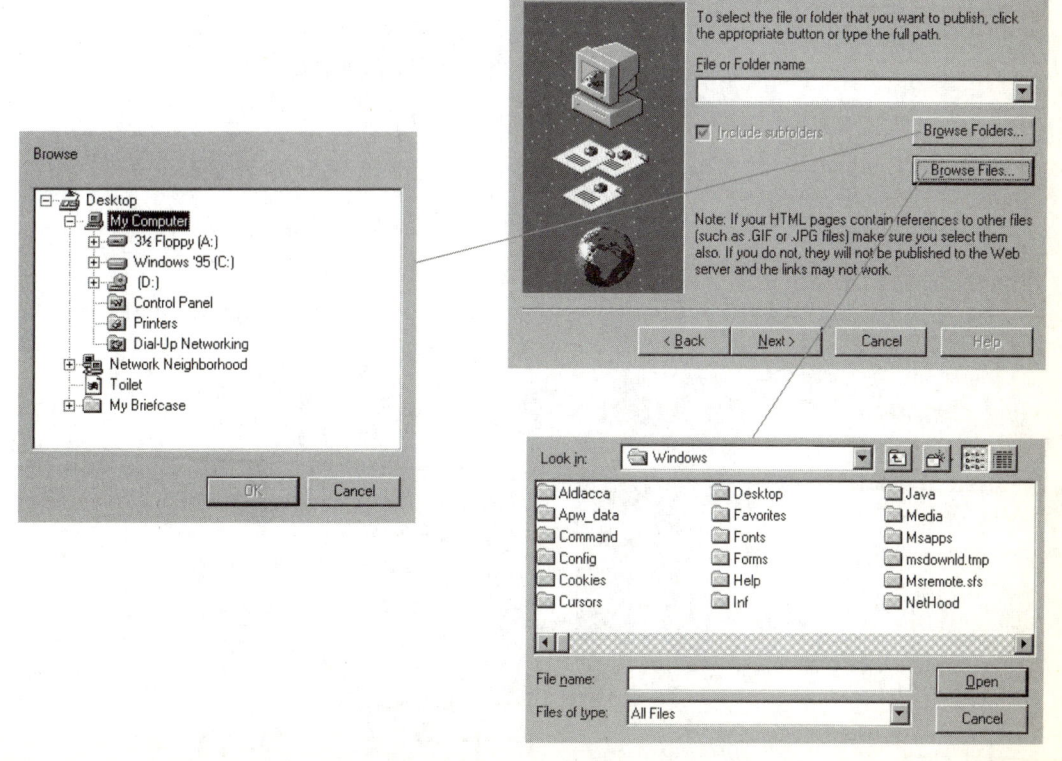

8. The Personal Web Server

...contd

4 Select the Web Server you want to publish your Web site to.

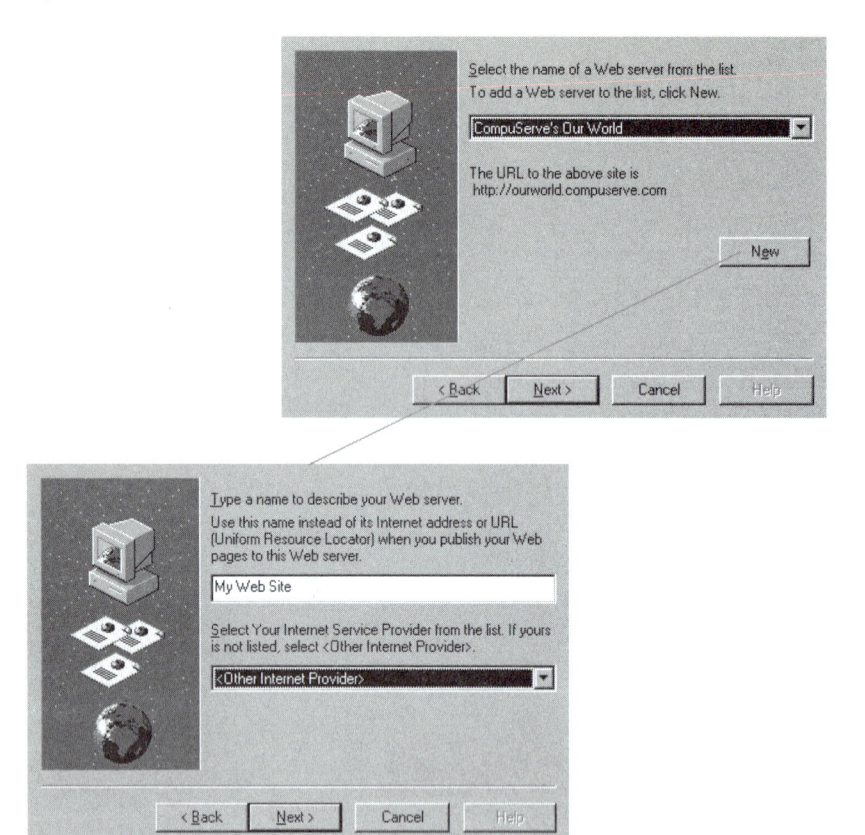

5 Enter the personal information requested and click Next.

152 FrontPage in easy steps

...contd

6 Enter the directory information requested and click Next.

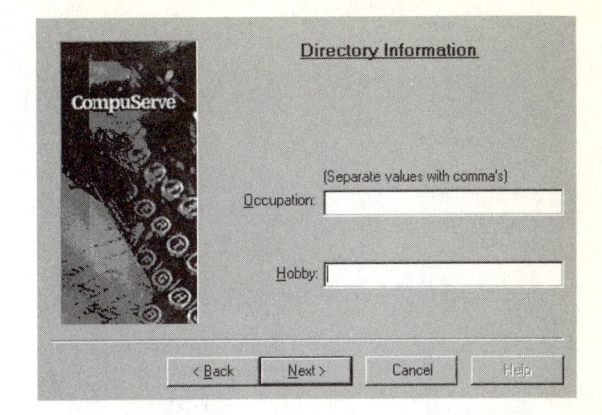

7 This account information would have been given to you when you opened your account. Enter it here and click Next.

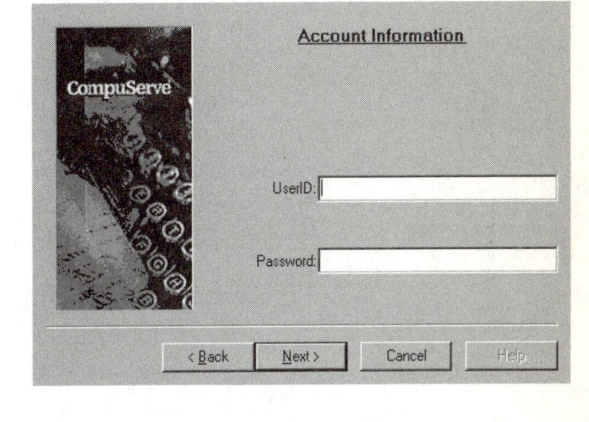

8 This is the last screen before FrontPage connects to your Server and begins to copy your Web site. Use the Back button to change any information you have given. If you are sure this is all correct, click on Finish.

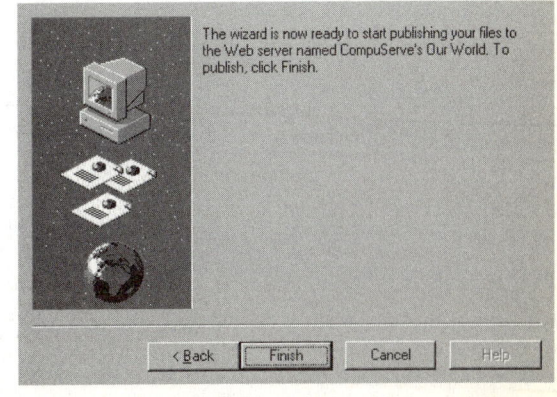

...contd

This is the most complex part of FrontPage that you will encounter as it links to your ISP and their server. The FrontPage Publishing Wizard is used to publish your Web to a server that does not have the FrontPage Server Extensions. As you know, if your server does have these already, the publishing of your Web site is a simple click of the mouse in the Explorer.

Many companies are now offering Web space on their servers for you to place your Web site on. Some offer to register and maintain your domain name as well. Shop around for web space. As with any commodity, you will find quite wide differences in the prices that you will pay for the same amount of space. Also, look closely at the services of ISPs other than the large providers such as CompuServe or MSN. If you already subscribe to one of these services you may get some free Web space, or a few megabytes of space for a small amount of money. To publish a small personal home page the free space may be enough to accommodate your site.

If it isn't enough, you will be charged usually by the megabyte of space that you lease from the provider. Of course, as this is FrontPage, only those providers that have the Server Extensions will offer you the most functionality with your Web site, as you will be able to use the WebBots you have placed on some of your pages.

Index

A

Access privileges 45-48
ActiveX icon 53
Add/Remove Programs 12
Adding files 33
Administrator 47
Alignment of text 90
Author 48

B

Bold text 90
Bulleted lists 90-91

C

Cell padding 54
CGI 125, 140
Character set 39
Check boxes 53, 129
Child Webs 147
Client Bots 104
Comments 57
CompuServe 154
Context help 24
Control Panel 12
Copy icon 51
Copyright 95
Corporate Presence Wizard 14-19, 88
Create FrontPage Web icon 23
Creating a Web site 14-20
Custom frames 70-72
Custom Grid 67
Custom templates 79-80
Customer Service Support Web (template) 88
Cut icon 51

D

Databases 17
Deleting a Web site 34
Discussion Web (Wizard) 88
Drop-down menus 53, 130

E

Editor 49-76
Editors, configuring 42-44
E-mail 29
Empty Web (template) 88
End User 48
Explorer 21-48

F

Fields. *See* Forms
File names 123
Find Words icon 23
Folder View 31-32
Formatting codes, Show/Hide icon 52
Forms
    Data Value 134
    Data Length 133
    Display Name 132
    Field Types 129-130
    Field Validation 131-134
    Fields 127-128
    Form Handler 135-138
    Form Page Wizard 122-126
    Handler, setting up 137-138
    Numeric Format 133
    Properties 135-136
    Text Format 132-133

Frames   67-72
Frames Wizard   67-72
FrontPage Publishing Wizard   149-154
FTP (File Transfer Protocol)   148

G

GIF (Graphics Interchange
    Format)   95, 101

H

Hotspots   99-100
HTML   61-63, 138
  Bulleted list   138
  Code   61-63
  Colour-coded   61
  Command   61
  Definition list   138
  Document   61
  Encoding (character set)   39
  Files, icon for   31
HTTP (Hypertext Transfer
    Protocol)   140
Hyperlinks   27-30
  Create/Edit Hyperlink icon   52
  Hotspots   99-100
  Show/Hide Hyperlinks Inside
    Pages   23
  Show/Hide Hyperlinks to Images   23
  Show/Hide Repeated Hyperlinks   23
  Verifying   41
  View   23, 27-30

I

Images   95-97, 99-101
  Files, icon for   31
  Hotspots on   99-100
  Insert Image icon   51
  Properties   97
  Transparent colours   101

Import Web (Wizard)   88
Importing documents   33
Indent, increasing/decreasing   90
Insert Plug-in icon   53
Installing FrontPage   8-11
Intranet   139
IP (Internet Protocol) address   37
ISP (Internet Service
    Provider)   139, 154
Italic text   90

J

Java - Insert Applet icon   53
JavaScript   104
JPEG (Joint Photographic Expert
    Group)   95, 101

L

Learning FrontPage Tutorial
    (template)   88

M

Mail   29
Marquee tags   58-60
MSN   154

N

New icon   51
Normal Web (template)   88
Numbered lists   90-91

O

One-line text boxes   53, 129
Open FrontPage Editor icon   24
Open icon   23, 51
Opening pages   93-94

P

Page properties   92
Page templates   78-80
Page Wizards   81-86
Password   14
   Changing   40
Paste icon   51
Permissions   45-48
Personal Web (template)   88
Personal Web Server   104, 139-154
Preview in Browser icon   51
Print icon   51
Project Web (template)   88
Publishing your Web site   145-154
Push buttons   53, 130

R

Radio button   53, 130
Redo icon   51
Refresh icon   52
Registration WebBot   119-120

S

Save icon   51
Scheduled Image WebBot   108-109
Scheduled Include WebBot   108-109
Scrolling text box   53, 129
Search WebBot   105-107
Server Administrator   142-144
   Authority security   144
   Checking extensions   143
   Installing extensions   142-143
   Uninstalling extensions   143
Server Bots   104
Server Extensions   104, 141
Settings, changing   35-39
   Advanced tab   38
   Configuration tab   37
   Language tab   39
   Parameters tab   35-36
Show Explorer icon   51
Show Folders icon   23
Show Image Editor icon   24
Show To Do List icon   24, 51
Sound, adding to Web pages   102
Spelling icon   23, 51
Starting FrontPage   13
Starting the Editor   50
Substitution WebBot   110, 113

T

Table of Contents   124
Table of Contents WebBot   114-116
Tables   54-56
   Insert Table icon   51
Template or Wizard dialogue   14
Templates   78-80, 87-88
Text   90-91
   Adding bullets/numbers to   91
   Alignment   90
   Bold   90
   Colour   90
   Files   73-76
   Italic   90
   Size, increasing/decreasing   90
   Underlined   90
Timestamp WebBot   117-118
To Do List   64-66
Toolbars
   Editor   51-53
   Explorer   23-24
Transfer   148
Transparent Colours   101

U

Underlined text   90
Undo icon   51
Uninstalling FrontPage   12
URL (Uniform Resource Locator)   115

V

Variables, adding   111-113
VBScript   104
Verifying hyperlinks   41
Video   98
View, changing   25-26

W

Web site
   Deleting   34
   Designing   89-102
   Viewing   22-24
   Visualising   27-30
Web templates   87-88
WebBots   103-120
   Client Bots   104
   Insert WebBot Component icon   51
   Registration   119-120
   Scheduled Image   108-109
   Scheduled Include   108-109
   Search   105-107
   Server Bots   104
   Substitution   110-113
   Table of Contents   114-116
   Timestamp   117-118
Whitespace   133
Wizards   81-86